PURE LOVE PURE LIFE

Exploring God's Heart on Purity

ELSA KOK COLOPY

ZONDERVAN®

ZONDERVAN.com/
AUTHORTRACKER
follow your favorite authors

Dedicated to some of the most amazing teens (and soon-to-be teens) in my life: Samantha, Rebecca, Mary, Hannah, Danielle, Mallory, Corie, Madison, Olivia, Heather, Bethany, Rachel, Emma, Sarah, and Maisey.

ZONDERVAN

Pure Love, Pure Life
Copyright © 2012 by Elsa Kok Colopy

This title is also available as a Zondervan ebook. Visit www.zondervan.com/ebooks.

Requests for information should be addressed to:
Zondervan, Grand Rapids, Michigan 49530

ISBN: 978-0-310-72609-8

Cover design: Gayle Raymer
Interior design: Sarah Molegraaf

Printed in the United States of America

11 12 13 14 15 16 17 18 19 /DCI/ 18 17 16 15 14 13 12 11 10 9 8 7 6 5 4 3 2 1

TABLE OF CONTENTS

ACKNOWLEDGMENTS

Wow, Jesus! If you can bring this kind of beauty from my kind of mess, I can't wait to see what you do in other lives! You are so good—thank you for this honor. And to my hunka-hunka-burning love, Brian K. Colopy. I'm so glad we do this pure life together—from when we were dating to our pure (to each other), crazy-in-love marriage. You are coolness and godliness wrapped in one studly package. I hit the jackpot with you! To my girl, Samantha K. Lynch, you were a huge catalyst to my pure pursuits. Thanks for reading this book, giving me good advice, and cheering me on. Love you, darling! Mom, thanks for being a prayer warrior and confidante—you're a great companion in this life. And to my fabulous editor—Jacque. Thanks for breaking me out of my stuffy voice and bringing me back to me. You rock! I also want to honor the special young woman (and her mom) whose story stirred my heart toward teens who have been violated. You know who you are—your story helped shape this book. And to the rest of my family for their support and cheers, I love you all: Dad (in heaven), Piet, Carol, Enno, Rob, Laura, John, Wendy, Linda, Brenda, Deb, Gary, Andrea, Chris, Joe, Tami, Dave, Jean, Kirk, Lori, Pieter, Luke, Caleb (in heaven), Ben, Curran, and Andrew. And finally, to Sean, Jessica, and Cassie: you're in my heart always. Oh, and I can't forget the pups: Reeses, who laid at my feet through the early writing of the book (faithful boy) and then went off to doggie heaven; Max, who chewed up the rough draft of the book (bad, but adorable boy), and Simba Roo, our skittish pup with a tender heart.

FOREWORD

We are eager to add our "Yea!" and "Amen!" to Elsa's book, *Pure Love, Pure Life*.

When we launched Teen Mania in 1986, it was with a deep desire to disciple teens toward transforming faith and radical love for our God and his people. God has been gracious in hearing the cry of our hearts. We have had the profound privilege of connecting with young people for almost twenty-five years now, and we have definitely seen it all! Unfortunately, we've seen over and over the effects of media and culture shaping the minds of our youth in the area of their purity and sexuality. From TV shows to Top 40 hits, the enemy has used captivating and clever antics to mold the values and morality of teenage America and the results have been disastrous!

Even our Christian young people who grew up in the church, who have caring Christian parents, are experimenting with the world's alluring ideas: "I kissed a girl and I liked it," "friends with benefits," "sexting," and more. The stats show that an overwhelming number of teens in the church are no different from the teens outside of the church. How can this be? So many Christian teens have been sucked into the same lies about sexuality as the un-churched kids and they're experiencing the same results—broken hearts and broken lives.

But the truth is, however captivating and seductive the world's ways seem, they do not work. If you think for a minute that they do, just look at Hollywood: the most "beautiful people" in the world, full of sex appeal and influencing millions, are some of the most broken, hurting individuals alive. What a dichotomy! They've got more money than they know what to do with, more fame, more popularity, more beauty (even if it is surgically induced), yet they go through marriages and relationships like they mean nothing at all. The cat fights, the drugs, the rehab, the turn-over in relationships, six marriages so far, and how old are they? Thirty-five?

And yet we watch their passionate romances on the big screens, and think "Oh, I want to be them!" They think they know what true love is? I don't think so!

Only God knows what true love is—he's the one who invented true love, true passion, marriage, and even sex. Think about that one—if you thought God was a religious, stuffy, antiquated old relic, you have the wrong idea about God. Sex was an original thought from God's heart. But he knows that sex doesn't work outside of a loving, covenant relationship between a husband and awife. As Elsa so eloquently states it, God does not give us boundaries to try to ruin our lives or to destroy our fun. He's trying to protect us from lies and inevitable consequences that really will destroy us in the end.

Elsa has written an incredibly down-to-earth, honest, and thought-provoking book to help you think through all of the issues you are bombarded with concerning purity and sexuality. She is a woman of integrity and cares deeply about your generation. As you read this book, you will feel the love and compassion God has for you no matter what you've been through, but you will also come to understand that his ways are very different from the world's ways.

If you truly desire wholeness in your life, long-lasting, healthy relationships with people around you, and maybe even an amazing marriage you've only dreamed about someday in the future, read this book! Fulfilling those dreams has everything to do with living a pure life before God.

One more thing: God never intended us to live this life alone and isolated. That's another reason why Christians fail to live a godly life; they're trying to do it on their own. We are meant to live in connection with other humans; in community—connected to friends who can cheer us on and hold us accountable; connected with mentors—older and wiser people who can give us wisdom and direction. (Elsa is one of those, mentoring you through her book.) We are also meant to be connected with younger people, to help them live life successfully. You can be an example for younger siblings and younger girls in your church. We are all examples to someone and we all influence others whether for good or for bad.

We want to encourage you to use this book in the most effective way. Gather a group of friends and read it together. Challenge each other. Discuss the ideas and hold each other accountable. Find an older godly woman who you can share your heart with and from whom you can gain wise counsel. If living out the ideas in this book is going to be a big change for you, you will need support and accountability to make those changes—but it will be well worth it—guaranteed!

We're so proud of you for picking up this book to read. It shows that you're seeking God's wisdom. 1 Timothy 4:12 says this: "Don't let anyone look down on you because you are young, but set an example for the believers in speech, in conduct, in love, in faith and in purity."

You have all that it takes to live this out!

Ron & Katie Luce

Founders of Teen Mania Ministries, Acquire the Fire, and BattleCry events with over three million in attendance, and Global Expeditions missions trips hosting 65,000 short-term teen missionaries.

INTRODUCTION

If I'd been born a pioneer woman—life in a buttoned-up dress, lacy bonnet, and sturdy boots—the only men who would have crossed my path would have been smelly, obsessed with gold, and completely disinterested in my dusty, tough-girl self. Without TV or a computer, I would never be exposed to what those smelly men may have looked like beneath their clothing. Keeping my heart focused on godly stuff would have been a breeze. What kind of girl thinks passionate thoughts or gets lost in racy images while trudging through six feet of snow to catch (and kill) a rabbit, field mouse, or muskrat for dinner?

Unfortunately, I was born into a world where guys smell good, searching for romance wins over muskrat hunting, and images assault me at every turn. The images were innocent enough at first. As a little girl, I loved watching all the happily-ever-after movies and TV shows. I would dream of my knight in shining armor—what he might look like, what kind of flowers he would bring as he rode in on his horse, that type of thing. So I began looking for him—everywhere. Louis was the first one to catch my eye. We were in the third grade. He was tall, I was tall. Obviously we were meant to be together forever. I used all my third-grade womanly wiles to get Louis's attention: I punched him in the arm, chased him at recess, and beat him in a contest to see who could jump the farthest off the swings. When I felt like I'd captured his heart, I let him know, in my gentle, womanly way, that it was time for us to take it to the next level and hold hands.

Maybe I moved a wee bit fast because Louis seemed to drift away after that. And then to add insult to injury, he asked Lisa—the only other tall girl in the class—to the school fair at the end of the year. I was crushed.

My next major love interest was Mr. Mooney. He was my sixth-grade teacher and he had a beard. With all the subtlety of a freight train, I wrote out my feelings to Mr. Mooney in a note. "I love your beard," I told him.

I think back now and can't help but laugh. I can almost picture him going home to his wife, proclaiming, "Look what Elsa wrote me today!"

My crushes started like that—harmless, innocent. But when Dominic took me behind the school to kiss me and then tried to look down my shirt, it freaked me out a little. I wondered, just for a second, if I might be in over my head.

When it came to kissing, touching, and sex, I was told what I *should* do: My parents encouraged me to stand for purity. My church told me to keep my hands to myself. Commercials told me to be smart and be good. Well, all the reasoning I heard from those authority figures seemed to fly out the window when boys like Gary leaned in to kiss me and spoke words that melted my heart: "You're so beautiful …" *Mmmm*, I thought. *Kiss me again!*

Besides, impurity seemed like a different kind of sin. I knew to stay away from drugs and alcohol and not to steal, kill, or lie. But then again I didn't wake up when I was ten years old wondering what it would be like to smoke pot or drink a beer. I didn't dream of stealing from the local department store. But I did wake up wondering what it would be like to kiss Louis. And the movies I watched didn't involve a princess sneaking off to smoke behind the castle or plotting how she would break into the royal liquor cabinet—I watched Disney movies where the strong prince scooped up the beautiful princess, kissed her, and rode off into the sunset.

To do what? I would wonder.

It was all so magical. And breathtaking.

Romance was good. Kissing was good.

But wait—sex was bad.

Holding hands, good. Hugging, good. But, hold on—doing any of that while steaming up car windows—bad.

These mixed messages littered my childhood, drenched my adolescence, and sidelined my teenage years. I got that I should stay away from drugs and alcohol. But romance? Love? Intimacy? How did that even compare? What did purity even mean? No French-kissing? No touching the "private" zones? No thoughts? It seemed far too confusing to put it all together so I didn't even try.

And then I fell in love. Darren fit the bill for the knight in shining armor I'd been looking for all those years. The love we shared was the most intense feeling I'd known. I couldn't seem to remember why it was so important to keep my hands to myself or wait until marriage to have sex. And where was *the* line again? In the middle of trying to figure it all out, we didn't do a lot to fight the temptations. Even though we were both Christians who had been taught differently, we ended up going further and further until ultimately, we had sex. We felt guilty at first, but that seemed to lessen as time went on. After all, we weren't really having sex, we were *making love*, and in my brain that made all the difference. Besides, I really couldn't see what the big deal was. Why was everybody so uptight about it? It's not like we were little kids. We loved each other.

I remember when my parents found out what we were doing. "You'll regret it," my dad told me.

"I'll never regret it!" I told him. "Never!"

And I'll be honest, for a long time I didn't. I loved Darren and nothing truly horrible happened the moment we slept together. Lightning didn't strike, the world didn't implode, I didn't stop loving God or suddenly grow horns and think evil thoughts.

So what *was* the big deal?

Then Darren broke up with me. We'd been dating for one year, and suddenly he thought we weren't going to make it.

I was devastated. I was crazy about him, and I didn't understand why he would walk away from something so good.

That's when things started becoming rough. I was miserable. I missed Darren so much and it literally took years to get over my broken heart.

At the time I thought it was because I was so in love with him. And yes, I loved him. But I understand now that something much bigger happened when we let ourselves go to different places physically. The more intimate we were, the greater the bond. And when we did have sex, we became one. Breaking that bond ended up breaking my heart.

And it was not pretty.

Then all the other consequences started filtering in. Feeling used. Disappointed with myself. The painful realization that I'd given away something I couldn't get back. I *thought* I was giving myself to the man I would spend the rest of my life with ... now, when I did meet that forever guy, I'd have to explain how I'd given myself to someone else. *Great.* And then came the temptation. Oh, wow. Since I'd gone there once, it was so tough not to just make the same decision over and over again. What did it matter now? I tried to rebuild what was lost, but I really had no clue what that even looked like.

I wish I could say that things turned around then. Well, they did, for a little while. I stayed away from guys of every shape and size for a season. But then Mike came into the picture. And then John. I had recommitted myself to waiting for sex until marriage, but my picture of purity was all messed up. I had it in my head that it was just saying no to sex. Do whatever you want, think whatever you want, spend time with whoever you want—but just don't have sex. It was a rule, and so I pushed its boundaries. Somewhere inside I wanted to be a "good" girl. I mean, it *sounded* like the right thing, but I still didn't know exactly what that looked like or, realistically, if I would ever be able to live it out

While I was really struggling to figure all that out, I met a Navy guy with blond hair, blue eyes, and a contagious laugh. Again, I let down my guard. We fell in love and our relationship became physical. I justified it because I was older and "Hey, we're *definitely* getting married." Unfortunately, because we had sex to turn to, we ignored a lot of the red flags in our relationship. We did get married, and had a beautiful baby girl. Only four years later, we went through a tragic divorce. My life seemed to unravel, and those childhood, romantic happily-ever-after dreams seemed forever lost.

I was sitting on a cement culvert in South Bend, Indiana, when it seemed like I finally woke up. I was a single mom of a toddler. I'd been through a divorce. I was sitting there smoking cigarette after cigarette. *This wasn't how things were supposed to turn out. This wasn't where my life was supposed to end up.* I was the one who was going to know the love of my knight in shining armor. We were supposed to live together forever—happy, goofy in love, fighting dragons, and making cute babies.

What had happened?

Oh, I was such a mess, and I stayed that way for a while. My picture of God was that he was probably disappointed in me. Angry. Distant. Done. In fact, that was another painful reality of going my own way for so long: I had no idea how to find my way back to God.

When I did decide to try to reconnect with him, it felt like I took one step forward, two steps back. Deep inside I was scared of his disappointment, so I would reach out to him for a little while, but then look for a guy to make me feel better. Then back and forth again and again.

Yet I couldn't stay away. I showed up at a small church one Sunday morning, reeking of cigarette smoke from being out the night before. I was nervous and I kept one eye on the door just in case things got weird and I needed to make a quick exit.

It was the pastor and his wife who headed me off before I could escape at the end of the service. They had nice smiles, and they shook my hand and looked me in the eye. They invited me over for lunch and asked me about my life. They didn't cringe or grimace or make faces. And they were nice to my daughter.

I decided I might like to go back.

That's how God worked with me. He was gentle. I was almost like a scared puppy, skittish and nervous. And he was like a dog whisperer. He didn't make any sudden moves. He held out his hand and waited for me to approach. In my timing and in my way.

I think that's when my faith went from memorizing Sunday school lessons to realizing there was a God who really loved me and cared about what happened to me. The more I got to know him, the more I realized how much *he* wanted to be my knight in shining armor, the love of my life. I realized he had always wanted me to live purely in order to protect me. He never wanted me to carry all that heavy stuff—guilt, pain, sadness, loneliness—that I was now lugging around. As I began to understand his heart, I figured out that, yes, he'd always wanted me to be pure, but not in an uptight, rigid, hate-guys kind of way. He wanted me to be pure by loving him and trusting him enough to let him map out my life, pick my guy, and protect me from getting my heart broken.

I was single for twelve years before I met the man God had for me. In that time I really started living purity more as an identity, a way of life, an understanding of God's love. I was learning more and more that it went beyond saying no to sex: it's what I think, do, see, and choose to experience. When I did start dating the man of my dreams, I was determined not to mess things up again. He was too. We dated, and the closer we grew, the tougher it was to hold on to our convictions.

I'd love to tell you, "Don't worry. Once you understand God's heart and make the commitment, the whole thing is a piece of cake." It's not even close. I was going to marry Brian, so obviously I thought he was sexy. And it's not like we shook hands with two feet of air between us at all times. We kissed and I confess (only to you) that sometimes I had a tough time not reaching for his tushie in the midst of our embrace. I wanted more. I wanted him.

So, no, it wasn't easy. And it won't be easy for you.

But it *is* worth it.

When I married Brian, I walked down the aisle in white. We had a wedding night that left us both breathless and delighted. It was beautiful. Just right. The whole process was really amazing. God had done these wonderful things in my heart as a single woman, helping me to love him in the coolest ways. Once I met Brian and we started falling in love, God gave us the supernatural strength to avoid ripping each other's clothes off prior to the wedding. And what I didn't expect was how purity isn't just a singles' thing or a dating thing, it's actually a marriage thing too. Brian and I stay pure in our love for God (not letting anything get in the way) and pure in our love for each other (not letting anyone else get in the way), and our marriage is incredible as a result. That may sound goofy and just the kind of thing I should say, but it's true. People roll their eyes when they listen to us talk or watch us interact. We're still stupid in love and a big part of that is because we both love God and we've fought through some of the toughest temptations together.

I want that for you. I want you to know the good things that choosing purity can bring—no matter where you've been, no matter your past, whether you've gotten it all right or struggled in an area or two. Listen, I *know* what it's like to pursue intimacy that feels good in the moment but ultimately turns south. I even know what it's like when the choice is taken away and someone touches you or takes a part of you that they didn't have any right to take.

I also know what it's like to feel God's love in a way that really changes things, and to live faith in the toughest moments of heartache or temptation. You can do this. You can learn to guard your heart, protect your body, and love God with all that you are.

But back to our pioneer woman. Maybe you, too, wish you lived in the days of buttoned-up beauty and smelly guys. But you don't. Guys today are anything but smelly. They're tough to resist. There are sexual images all over the place and temptation around every turn. So don't walk this road alone. Let me walk it with you and remind you that you are deeply loved, and that even if this is a broken area in your life, even if you are dealing with the painful consequences of your own choices or the cruel choices of another, God can heal and restore and rebuild. He is that good and he loves you that much.

So won't you join me? Will you walk with me along this road to purity of heart, mind, and body? It's a very difficult path and not for the faint of heart. But it is a road that will lead you to such amazing things. It's a road designed by God for your best, for your future—which holds so much more than you can even begin to imagine.

CHAPTER ONE

WHAT IS PURITY, ANYWAY?

Breaking it down

"I honestly don't know what God asks. I've been to many churches and I've gotten different responses. Most of them say something about living faithfully and being pure until you are married, but I'm not sure what they mean by that."

~Kaitlyn

THE BIG GIRL DEFINITION

I thought it might be interesting to check out the official definition of purity. Not that Dictionary.com is the author of truth, but it gave me a good picture. Here's what it says:

Purity is defined as:

> Freedom from anything that debases, contaminates, pollutes, etc.

> Freedom from any admixture or modifying addition.

Freedom from guilt or evil; innocence.

Physical chastity; virginity.

Freedom from foreign or inappropriate elements; careful correctness.

That's a whole lot of freedom. Freedom from guilt, contamination, and modifying additions. It's a neat thought—freedom. A life *free* from the things that mess with our hearts: shame, sin, pain, guilt. I actually get that. I carried pain and guilt for a long time after some of my choices. In fact, I still carry some regret, wishing I'd done things differently than I did. And when I was pressured to do things I didn't want to do, or for my friends who've been raped—yes, it would be great if we never had to carry any of that with us today. To be free would be an amazing thing. In fact, if that's your story, if you've been violated in any way, keep reading. You can still live this pure life out—you are not disqualified. We'll talk more about that in our "Second Chances" chapter, but for now, know that this book is not going to add to the pain you've already experienced. Hopefully, this book will only help you live the future you were always meant to have.

So purity *is* freedom. It's freedom from everything that can hurt you. But what else? Let's break it down into the everyday stuff of life. Throughout this book, we'll be looking at it from every angle: physical, emotional, and spiritual. Below is just a taste of what each of those angles can mean.

PHYSICAL

Physical purity is all about protecting your body, guarding it from hurtful things and saving it for good experiences. I know that makes sense on some levels, but it's tough to wrap your brain around it when you're in the middle of a temptation. Just like what happened in my relationship with Darren, kissing and touching didn't *feel* bad or hurtful in the moment. It's not like we started crossing lines and all of a sudden we were in pain and heartbroken. It was just the opposite. It felt good. We liked it. We had heard all the warnings, but we sure didn't feel like what we were doing was bad. I think that made us question all those people who told us to say no. They obviously didn't know what they were talking about, because holding each other didn't feel like a bad thing at all.

So I'm not going to tell you that if you kiss and touch and get more and more physical with your boyfriend, you'll keel over or turn purple or fall into some kind of abyss. You'll probably enjoy it in the moment; you just have to remember that it's the down-the-road consequences that God wants to protect you from. This is where trust comes in. God has good things for you. God knows that physical touch is a good thing. He created it. He designed it to bring us all kinds of pleasure, fun, joy. The only limit he put on physical connection is to let it happen in marriage. Why? Because someone who makes love to you in the evening should be there in the morning, and the morning after that—and that matters to God. Because you won't run the risk of disease that can be passed between two people having sex. Because you won't chance having a baby when you're not ready to provide. Because God knew that when you touch, caress, and hold another person, your heart is always involved, and he wants to protect your heart.

God is not some mean, uptight ogre in the sky looking

to keep you from having fun. He is good and kind, and he wants to protect you.

So then comes the question, how far is too far? What is the magical line, anyway? Exactly what can you do without walking into sin? When I surveyed girls, I got a few different responses:

> *"My line is holding hands. There is just something special even in that simple gesture. And it would be all the more precious if I save it for the man God has made for me. Also, I haven't officially decided, but it's always been in my mind that I would not kiss until my wedding day."* Mary

> *"I think going too far is having sex. My line stops at everything before having sex."* Jordan

> *"You've gone too far if you touch any area that a bathing suit covers."* Anonymous

> *"When I'm not in a serious relationship and completely in love with someone, it's easy to say no to everything. When I am in a relationship and we truly love each other, it is much harder and my line is pushed further back."* Anonymous

Notice how personal and unique each line becomes? That's because we're asking the wrong question. Unfortunately, whether your line is kissing or nothing below the belt, what will happen every time you're together with the person you're dating? You'll go right up to that line ... and then maybe push it back just a touch.

Ah, but then you'll feel bad and promise never to let it happen again.

Until next time.

Then you'll go right up to the line, and push it even further.

The frustrating thing about sexual lines is that you always want what you can't have. And you'll always be tempted to push back that magical line each and every time you're together. The things you do the first month of dating will lose their thrill, so in the second month of dating you'll push that line back a bit. By the third month of dating, the lines will have blurred even further. Pretty soon all those good reasons for guarding your purity as you date will be long forgotten as you become more and more consumed with what you want but can't have. Even the guilt will begin to diminish as you shed the "rules" and go with where you're sure your heart is taking you.

That's the danger of having a magical line that you dance around every time you're together with your date. You're basically putting yourself right smack into the middle of temptation and expecting your mind, body, and heart to listen to a rule you put in place what will feel like eons ago.

Think of it this way: Imagine that you're addicted to food, and that you have a special warm-fuzzy feeling when it comes to chocolate frosting. Now imagine that because of your deep love of frosting, you have decided to go into a bakery every single day. You determine to buy a slice of chocolate cake with the most decadent chocolate frosting ever. You put it down in front of you and begin to nibble at the cake portion. You even allow the frosting onto the fork, but then quickly put the fork down onto the plate. *See how strong I am?* You think to yourself, *I didn't even lick the frosting!* Of course you *did* stare at the frosting, play with the frosting, and imagine the taste of the frosting every single moment of nearly every single day. And then, sadly, the day comes: in a haze of frosting-induced obsession, you buy the entire chocolate cake and lick off every bit of frosting in sight. You even run around the counter and start licking off the tops of cupcakes. You simply won't be denied another moment.

This is the problem with asking the question "How far is too far?" It's like walking into the bakery and parking yourself in front of the cake case. The question you should be asking instead is "What can we do, as a couple, to think about other things? To *do* other things besides locking our lips and caressing each other's bodies?"

In other words, how can you stay out of the bakery all together?

Now, I'm not going to cheat you. I'll still answer the question as a starting point for you. It's my opinion that you shouldn't do anything beyond kissing. Some folks would say don't even go there. Talk to God, talk to godly people you trust, and once you have your answer, turn your focus to other things. That means avoiding sexting and flirting with words too, mainly because that's like describing the taste of the frosting down to the creamy, sugary deliciousness and not expecting your mouth to water. Your body will gear up for what your mind is thinking about and what your mouth is talking about. Again, it's best to just stay out of the bakery and turn to other things. The biggest part of your purity as a couple will be to work together to build your relationship through conversation and having fun together. Get outside. Play sports together. Go for a hike. Go to the movies or spend time with friends. Whatever you do, do yourself a big, huge favor and keep your eyes (and your hands ... and your thoughts) off the frosting.

EMOTIONAL

Emotional purity looks a whole lot like physical purity. It's protecting your heart—filling it up with good stuff and keeping hurtful things out. Again, it goes against the grain a little bit. Every show we've watched since we were little girls tells us that our happiness will come when we give our hearts away to the perfect guy: the sun will shine, birds will sing, all of life will fall into place. But again, it's a trust thing. Having a pure heart means loving God first, keeping other things out of the way, and letting God bring the guy (or trusting him to take care of us if it seems like the guy is taking *forever*).

It sounds so good and spiritual, but we all know it's not that easy. When a guy sweeps in who has that mischievous grin and warm gaze, it's hard to turn our eyes from his and look to the sky, stating, "My heart belongs to God."

Yeah. Not realistic, and kinda cheesy. But don't worry, having a pure heart that loves God isn't nearly as weird as it sounds. We'll look at what loving God really means as we wrestle through the coming chapters together. But for now, know that part of staying emotionally pure is loving God with abandon and keeping a good perspective on guys.

Emotional purity also deals with learning to handle other emotions. We'll talk about that more, but just as an example, you can imagine how feeling lonely can open the door to pornography—so it's good to know how to handle loneliness in a healthy way. Feeling love might open the door to compromise in your physical purity, so how can you enjoy feeling all the warm fuzzies with someone while still standing firm in your convictions? All those things tie into emotional purity as well.

SPIRITUAL

I have a different take on spiritual purity. Yes, of course it's loving God first and making sure we keep nasty stuff out of our relationships. In other words, it makes sense that watching pornography or having sex or fantasizing about stuff might distract you from God. But spiritual purity is more than keeping out the bad stuff; spiritual purity is all about pouring passion into good things. Again, we'll go into the details later in the book, but in short, instead of spending all your time thinking about the many things you don't want to do, it's pouring all that energy into good outlets. People underestimate the power of all that (positive) passion you have. I, however, believe in it. I can't wait to see what God does as he harnesses it and unleashes it on the world.

So that's the scoop. Purity is guarding your body, protecting your emotions, and pouring all that passion into great things. It goes against the grain, swims upstream, does things differently. It's amazing and it's a ride.

Interested in finding out more?

Let's start by looking at my mean math teacher. Oddly enough, he has something to do with this whole topic.

SO YOU DON'T CARE? FINE.

I didn't like my math teacher and I know for certain he didn't like me. He would always call my name with a sarcastic edge to his voice, as though he didn't expect me to know the answer and was just waiting for me to fail. Because I knew he didn't like me, I hated the class, barely did the work, and just scraped by with a passing grade.

Tiny Mrs. Weiner was a whole different story. She was small, but she was a spitfire. She was my creative writing teacher and she loved me. She'd smile wide when I walked in the door, we'd joke around, and she would write notes on my papers: "Way to go, Elsa—very creative how you made those green people jump out of the closet." Even on my worst papers, she managed to put a positive spin on her correction. "Nice try on the polka-dotted elephant dancing with a hula hoop, but you might want to stay closer to reality—perhaps make it a hippo." Not a huge surprise that I made sure to do the homework and aced that class.

It's amazing what a little love will do to our hearts. When we feel truly loved, there's little that we can't do— little we're not willing to do. Isn't that what can make some areas of purity so hard? You get into a relationship and you start falling for someone. You love him, he loves you. You wrap your arms around each other and it feels natural and right—it's about love or at least it's headed that way. Suddenly guarding your heart and your body doesn't seem as critical. *Why would I guard my heart from him?* we think. *He's a good guy, we're getting so close ...* We question it all, because of love.

But here is the truth: there is a greater love, and that's what most of us miss. As I surveyed teen girls and asked them why they think God wants them to stay pure physically and emotionally, it was all about the rules. "He wants me to obey him." "My body is a temple, so he wants me to keep it pure." "I'm not really sure. Because he said so." And it's true God says so ... and your body *is* a temple ...

but underneath is the bigger truth: God wants you to choose well because he loves you. He loves you more than you will ever know. He aches for you. He knows that by crossing lines physically or filling your mind with images, you could be deeply hurt, either by someone who doesn't stick around or by the images that might take away from a good relationship down the road. He doesn't ever want you to feel dirty or used or broken. God is a valiant knight, your first love, the one who knows you best and loves you most. He has a purpose in asking you to live differently and it's all for your good, because of *love*.

Do you believe you are loved by a good God? Ultimately, your decisions on purity will come out of what you truly believe. It's like the story of my math and creative writing teachers. When I felt unloved, my commitment to the teacher was nonexistent. When I felt believed in and cared for, my desire to please my teacher grew by leaps and bounds. So it is on a much larger scale with our God. If you believe God doesn't love you or that he's angry and distant—like an uncaring teacher watching your every move and expecting you to fail—then you aren't going to want to stay pure.

God asks us to live pure lives. I don't know exactly why, but he has every right to lay down the rules for us to follow. It's our responsibility to follow them, period.

~Anonymous

On the other hand, if you know that God is perfect, kind, and good—and that he is crazy about you, believes in you, and delights in who you are—you'll be a whole lot stronger when the temptations come your way. You'll already *know*

you are loved. You'll trust that your perfect God has something better for you, and even when it's a monster struggle
(and it will be at times), you'll be much more equipped to win
the fight. Now, I'm not saying that God's love is a magic wand
in that all of a sudden you'll stop thinking about sex or guys
or that you'll immediately turn away from a tempting image
… but God's love will give you a stronger foundation, a better
reason, a more convincing motive to make the hard choices.

This was exactly my journey. I knew God wanted me to
make choices toward purity, but I didn't really know who
God was, or how much he loved me. I pictured God as a stern
man in the sky—in my brain he had a white beard, stood
with his arms crossed, and had a look of harsh disappointment in his eyes. Kind of like my math teacher, I figured God
expected me to fail. He loved me because he had to, but he
probably didn't like me very much. Since that was my mindset, physical purity was a rule that I stuck with for a while,
but when love entered the picture in the form of a handsome
guy, I ended up giving in to temptation—and paid the price
of a broken heart. Later, as I grew in my love for God and my
understanding of his character and his love for me, everything changed. When I fell in love with Brian, we both had
that foundation of God's love in place. So when those physical temptations came—when Brian wrapped his arms around
me and his lips lingered on mine, when all we wanted to do
was take it to the next level—that little voice reminded us of
God's heart behind it all. Granted, we had to put all kinds of
safeguards in place—we needed help to keep from touching
all the wrong things and thinking all the wrong thoughts—
but it was that voice, that constant reminder of a greater love,

that made it even remotely possible for us to stay physically pure while we were dating.

> **"I get inspired by the idea that God has my best interests in mind. I figure he wouldn't want us to wait unless there was something amazing to wait for."**
> *~Anonymous*

UMMM, HOW?

It sounds good, but how do we feel loved by God? How do we make it more than about the rules, and how do we build that relationship so that when temptation comes we can do a better job of escaping it? That's exactly what we're going to look at in the next chapter—not how to know more stuff about God, but how to see him, experience him, and love him in real ways. You'll hear about some things God did to meet girls just like you, right where they were. These are the things I love about God—how he gets in our faces with his love and it can't help but change us. But first, look at the discussion/journal questions at the end of the chapter. Answering these will help take all this stuff from your head to your heart. It works best if you're doing this in a group, so you can process how to apply it in life—plus, it's just fun to talk through these things together. But if you can't do it in a group, pull out a journal and work through the questions, maybe tackling one chapter a week. It will help bring it all home.

DISCUSSION/JOURNAL QUESTIONS

Before you opened this book, you had a definition of purity in mind. What did purity look like to you?

As we explored purity in three different ways (physical, spiritual, and emotional), did your original definition change at all? Share the ways your thinking may have shifted.

Can you see how knowing you are loved by God (really, really knowing) might make a difference in your choices regarding purity? Why or why not?

CHAPTER TWO

CLOSER THAN YOU THINK:

Seeing God's love
(and letting it make a difference)

Samantha was a wreck. It had just been one of those days. Her friends were acting weird, finals were just around the corner, her boss was planning to cut her hours, and her boyfriend had just quit responding to texts.

"What's wrong?" she'd asked him three different times. Nothing, no answer. He always responded to texts, so what was going on? Was he mad? She tried to think over their last conversation. She didn't think she'd said anything wrong ...

I don't get this, God, she said as she drove home. *Why does it always happen all at once?*

Samantha walked in the door of the house and fell onto the love seat. Her parents were out and the emptiness felt tangible. Tears slipped over and spilled down her cheeks.

"Why does everything always have to be so hard? It would really help if I could feel you right now," she said to the ceiling.

Her dog, Simba Roo, padded into the living room. Since he'd been abused as a puppy, he didn't usually get too close. And on a normal day, that wouldn't matter. Samantha watched as Simba Roo crossed the room and stood in front of her.

"Hi, Simba Roo," she said through her tears.

Simba put one paw on Samantha's knee. Then the other on her opposite knee. Samantha sat up straighter as Simba squatted on his haunches and jumped onto Samantha's lap.

"Simba Roo!" Samantha gasped as Simba settled against her chest and tucked his head over her shoulder. The tears came again and Samantha wrapped her arms around Simba Roo and pressed her face into his fur.

"He's never done this," Samantha whispered to the ceiling. "He's never done this before!"

Sam cried—partly from the bad day, partly from the love that she knew God was giving her through Simba Roo. She cried until there were no more tears.

God will use everything at his disposal to show us how much he loves us. He gave his Son, he gave us this world with all its beauty, and he enters our every day. Sometimes we box God up and make our relationship with him all stiff and formal. He's not stiff. He's not formal. He's not somewhere far away on a throne.

He's specific and right there in your world.

"I don't get it," a friend once said to me. "How can God love us like that when he has a zillion people to take care of? You're trying to tell me that he shows up in my day when he's supposed to love all those other people too?"

Yes, that's exactly what I'm saying.

It says in Psalms that God knows the number of hairs on your head. If he's not too busy to know how many hairs are on your head, how could he possibly be too busy to love on you through your puppy? Through a sunset? Through a friend?

When I was single (for an eternally long time), I hated Valentine's Day. Worst holiday ever. Oh, I tried to have a good attitude about it, but it always seemed that by the end of the day I was grumpy, miserable, and just plain ticked off.

To make matters worse, I always seemed to be surrounded by people who were either dating or married—and annoyingly happy about it. They'd come around and pity me, sometimes giving me a flower from their dozens or offering me a chocolate from their box of ten thousand. Of course, it was usually the wilted flower or the chocolate with coconut ...

Not that I'm bitter.

One Valentine's Day, I was journaling about the whole thing. In my journal, I talked to God. I told him how I didn't like the day. I told him that I was having a really bad attitude and I was kinda hoping he would forgive me for it. Finally, feeling incredibly goofy and overly sentimental, I wrote, "God ... will *you* be mine?"

I shut the journal and quickly tucked it under the couch.

I went about my day.

I received the wilted flower and the coconut chocolate and felt a little like punching someone.

Finally, I came home. My neighbor came to her door and said, "Elsa, something came for you today!"

"Really?"

I grinned from ear to ear as I looked at the rose and vase in her hand. I took it from her and opened the small card.

It said: "Will you be mine? I love you. God."

My jaw dropped. Tears came to my eyes.

Seriously? God sent me a rose?

I hadn't told a single soul about what I wrote in my journal. How had this happened? Now, do I think that God went down to the florist and asked them to send a rose to Elsa over on Brewer Drive?

I guess he could have ... but I'm thinking he put it on someone's heart to reach out to me like that. However it happened, it totally blew me away. He answered my prayer. He answered my prayer very specifically. And I've never forgotten it.

I call those little moments when God shows up in our world God kisses. They come in painful moments, they come in lonely moments, they come when we least expect them, but they come when we need them the most. You might see the most beautiful sunset when you've had a rough day, or a friend might reach out and hug you when the tears are right there at the surface. Maybe a song will come on the radio, or you'll open up your Bible to read a verse and it will remind you that God has you in his hand.

Once you start looking for them, God kisses won't always look like you think they will. Sometimes I've asked God for something and it seemed like my voice just echoed into nowhere. I'd hear stories like the ones I just shared and wonder if maybe I just didn't have the touch, that maybe God would do that for others, but not for me. The key is to know that God hears your prayers, he hears your heart, and your feelings matter to him. He will always respond; it just might not look like you expect. He is a good God with a mind of his own who gets very creative when it comes to loving his children. God is there. He is speaking. That's why it's so important to ask him to give you eyes to see his hand in your life, because when you look, you'll see God kisses everywhere.

CALLING OUT

So what if you've never noticed a God kiss in your world before? What if you're not sure about the God thing, or you struggle with doubts? If you and I were sitting across the table, and we were diving into the world's best dish of chocolate ice cream (with chunks of chocolate), lathered in whip cream and sprinkles, I would tell you how I've been there too. I'd let you know that it's okay to have doubts, it's okay to wrestle in your relationship with God. It's okay to be skeptical and uncertain about what it all looks like.

Just be real with him. God already knows what's going on in your heart, so be real and tell him what you're thinking and feeling. I can remember doing exactly that. I didn't think that I loved God and I told him so. I told him as tears streamed down my face. "I don't love you, but I *want* to." I had my doubts and I knew that I'd just been going through the motions, that my faith was pretty shallow. I couldn't even seem to follow the rules that were supposed to make me good: don't cuss, drink, smoke, or have sex. I spent a lot of time trying, pretending, and lying about who I really was—and it never felt right. I finally turned to God, tired of faking it, and said, "God, I want the real thing. I've seen people who are crazy about you, who smile and it's real. They say they love you and they seem to mean it—they live it. I've also seen people who say they're Christians, but they're some of the meanest people around. They're uptight and annoying—or they say they're Christians and live a totally messed up life. If I'm going to do this, if I'm going to call myself a Christian, I want the real thing. I want to love you with all my heart. I want to know your love for me. I want to know who you are and I want you to know me. I don't want to fake it and not feel a thing. I don't want to act good or try to seem all religious. I want relationship with you and I want it to be real!"

Believe me, it was amazing what God did with that prayer. It wasn't immediate. It didn't happen overnight, but over time, my relationship with him became real and true. Yes, sometimes an unhealthy guy would come into my world and those real arms would draw me away. Other times a temptation would sideline me for a while. But eventually, the more I knew God and experienced his love, and the more I spent time with his people, the closer we became—and he began changing me from the inside out. I've been walking with God for a while now, and it's such a good thing. So I want to give you hope. It won't always feel like you're taking one step forward, two steps back. As you are real with God and tell him what you're thinking and feeling, as you ask him to show you his love, as you learn about him and love him, you'll begin to see how much he cares about everything in your life. And when you see that, you'll have more strength to face the tough temptations because you'll know that he has your back.

So talk to God. If you're struggling with seeing his love, ask him to give you eyes to see it. If you're not sure you even want to live this pure life we're talking about, ask him to help you understand why it matters and ask him for the heart to live it out. Wherever you are today, call out to God. Be real. Be authentic. Tell him your heart and watch how he responds.

When they cry out to me, I will hear, for I am compassionate.

Exodus 22:27

He fulfills the desires of those who fear him; he hears their cry and saves them.

Psalm 145:19

LOOK

After you call out to God, look for him. Look for him in the Bible, in the words of your family and friends, in songs, in circumstances, in nature. Make room for the reality that he might show himself in different ways, but keep your eyes out for those God kisses and when you see them, sit in the moment and let yourself receive that love.

And don't forget the biggest God kiss any of us have ever received: Jesus giving his life for us.

Now don't tune me out. I can remember hearing how Jesus loved me, how he gave his life for me, and I would tune out whoever was talking. For a long time, those were just religious words to me, not something that made a difference in my life. It was tough to make the reality of his love move from my head to my heart. One day I was listening to some worship music on a walk. A song came on, and the lyrics talked about when Jesus went to the cross: *Like a rose trampled on the ground, you took the fall, and thought of me. Above all.* I quickly fast-forwarded to the next song. This one made me uncomfortable. Thought of me? Doubtful.

I stopped walking and looked out over the lake. *What if he did?* The thought came to mind, and it felt like Jesus spoke to my heart: *What if I did think of you that day, Elsa?* My heartbeat quickened. The thought that me, and my face, may have come to his mind that day—suddenly it became so real.

Your smile. Your eyes. What if it was your face that strengthened him to take the next step with that heavy cross on his shoulders? What if the very knowledge that you would say yes to faith one day gave him the strength to give his life? What if he held on to your image in his mind as they put the nails in his hands? Knowing that by saying yes to belief in him, you would be strengthened in this life and spend all eternity in heaven with him?

You, his daughter.

Knowing that kind of love is one giant step toward living out this life we've been talking about. You'll face temptation—that's part of the human ride. But knowing that you are loved, and how big that love is, will strengthen you. So no matter where you are in your relationship with God today, ask him to take you one step closer. (And if you've never asked Jesus into your life, or you're not sure what that means, check out the "Do you know Jesus?" section on page xx for all the details.) No matter where you are in your relationship, ask to see God's hand and then look for those God kisses. Let him love you, and let that love strengthen you. Then read all the rest of the stuff in this book to help you live the life you want to live. Because there's more. You'll need people, tools, good things to think about.

But we'll get to that. In the meantime, here are some Bible verses to help remind you of his love. Take these verses and put them somewhere you can see them. It might be the reminder you need just when you need it.

> The LORD will fight for you; you need only to be still (Exodus 14:14).

> For God so loved the world that he gave his one

and only Son, that whoever believes in him shall not perish but have eternal life (John 3:16).

For I am convinced that neither death nor life, neither angels nor demons, neither the present nor the future, nor any powers, neither height nor depth, nor anything else in all creation, will be able to separate us from the love of God that is in Christ Jesus our Lord (Romans 8:38-39).

When I said, "My foot is slipping," your unfailing love, Lord, supported me (Psalm 94:18).

"I know my God loves me more than any man could ever love me … and that he will never walk away."
~Brittany

DISCUSSION/JOURNAL QUESTIONS

So let's make this real. This is not about Sunday school or showing up at church or being a good girl so your parents will be happy. This is about the God of the universe entering into your world and changing everything with his love. For your discussion/journal time, read the following letter. It is based entirely in Scripture. But before you read a word, ask God to show you his heart for you. Right this second. Close your eyes, ask to see and feel his words as you read this letter. Then answer the questions for your discussion/journal time.

Dear (your name here),

I love you. You are mine. I made you. I know every hair on your head and every worry in your heart. I know your hurts and your dreams. I was there through all the joys of your childhood and in the sorrows that broke your heart. I loved watching you smile and ached with you when you cried.

You have never been alone and you will never be alone. I love you with an everlasting, unchanging, heart-pounding love. I have a purpose and a plan for your life, and I will walk with you every step of the way. Will you trust me? I want relationship with you. I want to protect you. I want you to know how much I love you and how I will never abandon you or walk way. Not ever. Nothing can separate you from my love.

Be real with me. Talk to me. Yes, I know what you're thinking and feeling, but I love to hear your voice. So talk to me, and then look for me. See my love in the sunset and sunrise, in a friend's hug or a warm breeze. Feel my love through my people, music, all of creation.

I love you.

God

(To see the Scriptures covered in this letter, check out: Psalm 139:13; Matthew 10:30; Psalm 139:23; Psalm 56:8; Hebrews 13:5; Exodus 15:13; Jeremiah 29:11; Romans 8:39; John 14:23; Psalm 33:5; Psalm 90:14.)

Have you ever been real in your relationship with God? Sharing your fears, doubts, or worries? If you haven't, would you be willing to give it a try? Why or why not?

Share a recent God kiss.

When you read the letter from God, how did you feel? Were you able to believe it, or did it just feel like more religious words? What do you think might help you build your relationship with God in a way that would make a difference in your life?

CHAPTER THREE

THE GOOD STUFF

Benefits of choosing purity

The fight is hard. The temptations are tough to deal with. So what's the payoff? Let's take a little time to look at the good things that can come from saying yes to God in the purity area of our lives. Here, we'll break it down into the benefits you'll see in your dating relationships, and then in your personal life. Later on in the book we'll talk about the amazing things that purity can bring to marriage. Good stuff across the board!

PURE DATING

Purity makes a huge difference when a relationship turns steamy. But before we dive into that, let's be specific about what purity looks like within the context of dating. Like we said early on, it's more than just saying no to wandering hands or sex itself. It's living your love for God in the good things you pursue. It's guarding what you think about, what you look at, and what you communicate through other forms of connection (cell phones, pictures, instant messaging, texting, etc.). Remember, if you fill your brain with images from a computer screen, it makes it tough not to cross lines physically. If you flirt in sexual ways by phone or via the Internet, you're likely to push the line when you're together. Living in purity is the whole package, and choosing purity will help you across the board in your dating relationship.

BENEFIT ONE: *You find out about the guy you are dating*

Lips are good. Strong biceps are good. Arms wrapped around you while smooching—feels good. Trying to figure out the brain, heart, and character of the guy underneath those lips and muscles—nearly impossible if you don't ever come up for air.

It's just the way it is. It's easy to get distracted when the physical part of your relationship starts taking over. When kissing goes on for hours or every disagreement turns into an opportunity to kiss and make up, it gets really easy to lose sight of what might be happening in other parts of the relationship.

There were a few times in my life where I would have laughed at that. What do I care about his character? I just want to date someone I like, kiss a bit, and enjoy—I'm not planning to marry the guy! But here's the thing. We may think it's no big deal to go from guy to guy. We might even define ourselves as modern women with a modern I-could-care-less take on relationships and romance.

> *Not me. I won't get caught up and give away my heart.*

> *I won't lose sight of the big picture or get carried away and do something I'll regret.*

I'll be the girl to keep her cool, and her perspective and heart in line.

It's what we all think. Teens a hundred years ago thought they were the modern teens of the day, and ran straight into a twisted romantic mess.

Character matters. Heart matters. Faith matters. And there's no such thing as a casual dating relationship. Every time you spend significant time with someone, every time you allow physical stuff to happen, you're building something. You are connecting your heart to his, and for better or worse that interaction will affect your life. So when you allow a relationship to be all about the physical, it tends to blind your sight when it comes to who the guy really is. If he kisses well, you might not notice that he's mean to his friends. He might be rude to your parents, but because his strong arms feel fabulous when they are wrapped around you, you look past that glaring reality. And maybe you fight a little too much or don't share anything in common, but the way your lips fit together … wow.

Ultimately, the character stuff will come out. The heart issues will spill out on you, and you'll pay a price down the line. A dishonest guy will lie to you. An unfaithful one will find someone else who makes him feel better. A selfish guy will expect you to do whatever it takes to make him happy. If you ignore those big things because your lips fit well together, the consequences can be huge.

The flip side is that you may be dating a good guy with amazing character. A few dates in, you find out he's a great kisser and has strong biceps, and you start letting yourself get lost in his kisses. Both of you are missing out if you focus solely on the physical side of your relationship. Let him find out about the heart of you, who you are underneath your kisses. Let him discover the things that make you unique and amazing. Give him the chance to see who you are inside by setting some boundaries, and give yourself the same gift by taking the time to know the incredible guy behind the biceps.

So a huge benefit of purity when dating is *clear vision*. By keeping your dating relationships from getting too physical, you get to know the heart and character of the guy you are dating—and he gets to know you. The results can be so worth the wait. You might find out you really enjoy his sense of humor, or that you both like pizza with extra pepperoni (but no olives). You might find out that he secretly loves Disney movies or that he's always dreamed of being a police officer in New York City. You might discover that he loves to clobber guys in football, but is a huge pushover when his dog wags his way to his feet, jumps up, and slobbers his face.

Those biceps and lips are attached to a young man making his own way in this broken world. And if he is a young man of faith, you'll get to find out the coolest things as you set the physical aside. If he's not a guy sold out in his faith, you'll quickly find (before you get too deeply attached) that he isn't a good match or a good outlet for your admiring glances, warm encouragement, and gentle kisses.

Keeping clear vision is a *huge* benefit—both protecting you from the guy with majorly rough edges and giving you the chance to really love the one with the great heart and fabulous biceps.

BENEFIT TWO: You know the guy is sticking around because he genuinely likes you

Every time he laughs, his dimples crater out. He's got the

best smile, tousled blond hair, and piercing blue eyes. The more you get to know him, the more you like him. He tells you that he's a Christian and that he's trying to live a godly life. He wants to stay pure, he wants to honor you, and he wants to honor his God. "It's not that I'm not attracted to you," he says, and you can tell from the way his face flushes red that he means it. "And I can't say that I'm not tempted … but I really want to get to know you as a person." He asks what you like, what you think, what you're passionate about, and what makes you mad. He tells you that you're smart and beautiful, kind and funny. The more you spend time with him, the more you figure out that he cares deeply about your heart and he's protective of your purity.

It feels amazing.

Imagine it. As you get to know someone, as you start dating, you don't have to question motives. You can trust that this guy is spending time with you because he genuinely likes you for who you are. You can know that he values you as a person and you don't have to question if he's just hanging around for physical touch. Not that you won't struggle with temptation—both of you—but at least you'll know that underneath the battle lies a heart that really wants to do the right thing.

What an awesome thing!

At least it sounds awesome … but I have to confess something. I remember being scared about this particular truth. There was a part of me that didn't think a guy would stick around if I didn't get physical. Sure, it sounded good when people told me how nice it would be to be loved for me, but they forgot to address the bigger question: would somebody actually love me for me? Was there anyone really willing to wait for physical touch, and was I enough without it?

If you're in that place I know I can't convince you otherwise in just a few paragraphs, but my prayer is that you'll hear me on this: you are worth waiting for. You don't have to give yourself away, you don't have to lose yourself in the physical to hide from being rejected. If that's your fear, please talk to God about it, please ask him to help you see yourself differently, and ask him for the courage to let someone love you for you.

You are worthy of this type of relationship—one where you are honored, cared for, and protected for who you are as a person.

"If you make pure choices when you're dating, you'll feel good about the relationship and know that the guy likes you for you and not only for your body."
~Emily

I DON'T BUY IT ...

"Guys have needs," Beth told me. "Whenever I get into a dating relationship, that's what the guy tells me. It's like he'll explode or something if I don't do something with him."

"It's all guys seem to want," another teen shared with me. "I haven't dated one guy who doesn't make a big deal out of the physical. I wouldn't even know how to be in a relationship without some kind of physical stuff happening."

So what's the real scoop? Will guys explode if you don't take care of their physical needs?

No, they won't explode, but if they haven't learned much about their own bodies, they might think they will. See, guys *are* wired differently in that they have to fight sexual urges all the time. Their mind goes there quickly and it can be tough for them to keep those desires at bay. Unfortunately, there aren't a lot of books out there to help them figure out how to control their desires and still love the girl they're with. So what's your responsibility? First, understand that it isn't easy for them, even as you set healthy boundaries. In other words, don't think he's a complete jerk because he thinks a lot about the physical stuff. But also remember that understanding his wiring doesn't mean you have to give in to his desire, or to your own.

Secondly, there are guys out there (even guys who profess to be Christians) who know they can wait, but just don't want to ... They are so focused on the physical that they push and push, leaving a string of hurting girls in the dust behind them. Stay away from that type of guy, the one who might guilt you or shame you into going places you don't want to go. "I have needs," he might say, with the full expectation that it's your job to fill them.

It's not your job to "take care" of a guy physically, and if you ever feel that from a guy you are dating, make sure to take a step back and reevaluate the relationship.

Finally, please know there are guys out there who get it, who understand purity and value women. They want to do it right. They want to honor you and they are doing their best to live out purity in how they interact with you.

I know several young men who are choosing well. I asked one of them, Ben, to share his heart with you.

Dear Future Wife,

I am here and I am waiting. I am waiting for the girl that God has for me, the girl I'll love for the rest of my life. I am waiting for you. Will you wait for me?

There are a lot of rough guys in this world who want to use up and spit out innocent girls. I pray with all of my heart that they won't do that to you as well. Those kind of guys don't care about your feelings as much as what they can get you to do with them. I am not like that. I am waiting for you because I want to love you for who you are. I want to see you the way God sees you: his beautiful creation. I want to really get to know you: your likes and dislikes; your favorite dessert; your hobbies; everything.

Now not all guys are evil or out for sex. There are some who really think they are in love. They want to take the relationship to the next level physically because they think that's what's supposed to happen. But they're wrong. Real love keeps your best interests at heart. True love respects your purity and your beliefs. In fact, if he really loved you the way God loves you and the way I would love you, he would encourage you in your quest for purity. Think about it: if he doesn't have your best interests at heart or doesn't honor your purity, then how can that be love?

Please wait for me. I am ready to spend the rest of my life with you. Please don't give your heart or your body away to another man. Guard your heart and your mind. I am waiting for you, and God is preparing my heart to give my everything to you.

Love,

Your future husband

(To read about other guys standing for purity, visit www. purelovepurelife.com and click on the "Guys Who Care" section under "Teens only.")

The young man who wrote this letter is sixteen years old. He's tall, handsome, and intelligent. He loves adventure and is devoted to our God. He and others like him are waiting for you; will you wait for them?

Will you say no to the others who would take what you offer and walk away?

You are worth waiting for, you are worthy of guarding your purity. Don't settle for anyone who wouldn't treat you exactly in that way. That's the kind of love God wants for you. That's why he's been protecting you. He has so much more for you than cheap sexuality. He has pure, powerful, and beautiful intimacy in mind for you—first with him, then (if marriage is your desire) with your future husband.

> **"I'd be so inspired in living purity if I could just be with someone who wants to have fun hanging out, instead of being with someone who wants to get to first base, then second, so on and so forth."**
> **~Skye**

BENEFIT THREE: You don't have to worry about diseases or pregnancy

Imagine living totally worry free ... If you keep yourself

physically pure, saying no to sex or any other act that exchanges bodily fluids, you don't risk pregnancy or any other sexually transmitted disease. That's huge. When you're sexually active, there's no guaranteed protection against pregnancy or disease. Birth control can fail, condoms can tear, things can happen that leave you vulnerable to life-changing consequences.

Too many girls have spent days, weeks, and months worried about what might have happened when they crossed that line. *Am I pregnant? Did I catch something? What happens if he gave me some kind of disease?* It's a lingering fear that can suck the joy right out of your world. Don't underestimate the benefit of living totally free from that worry.

> **"I would kiss a boy only if I really liked him, after getting to know him gradually. I definitely wouldn't go any further than that."**
> *~Anonymous*

BENEFIT FOUR: That better-than-Christmas feeling

"Two months, three days, and two hours," Jett said to me.

"Two months, three days, and two hours until what?"

"Until I get married ..."

Jett's eyes were shining and he was looking across the room at his fiancée. She caught his eye and smiled back. I knew the two of them were committed to purity, so it was fun to watch their interaction and know how the anticipation was building. It reminded me of Christmas.

I was ten years old and I knew I was going to get cowboy boots. I was so excited that I made a calendar and literally crossed off not the days, but the hours until the big moment. The anticipation itself was almost as thrilling as actually opening the gift and pulling out those cowboy boots. Oh, and when I did—I wore those boots with every single outfit for every single day.

My dream had finally come true and I couldn't get enough.

An amazing benefit to keeping your body pure while dating, and your heart pure and focused on God, is the fun of looking forward to the wedding day. Not only will you be married, but you get to experience a whole new level of intimacy with your man. The anticipation builds, the excitement grows—you count down the hours and so does he.

Better than looking forward to Christmas. Better than any birthday gift you ever anticipated. Unwrapping the gift of each other's bodies, exploring and enjoying—and all under God's total and complete blessing.

That kind of pleasure is worth fighting for.

BENEFIT FIVE: You find out you're stronger than you ever thought

Living pure is living strong. Every time you set a boundary for yourself by getting out of the car, choosing not to respond to a steamy instant message, turning away from a computer image, or changing the course of a racy daydream, you are building strength in your purity. At first, it may feel nearly impossible to say no or to turn away—almost like lifting a weight in the gym and finding that your arm gives under the strain. But the more you work it, the more you refuse to give in, the stronger you become. The only time this doesn't apply is when you're in a relationship and the attraction deepens over time. Then the temptation can actually get stronger. Keep this in mind though: as you show yourself that you have what it takes to set a boundary and stick with it in the smaller things, you'll be able to stand firm in those temptations that get more intense over time.

I can't may be your very first thought. *It's too hard. It's all around me. My friends talk about things, TV is all about it, my thoughts keep going there ... I can't do this!*

Oh, but you can! Because you are not in this alone. It's as if you have a huge body-building champion standing behind you as you try to lift the heavy weight. The minute your muscle starts to shake, he steps in and lifts it the rest of the way. Just breathing the words *God, help me* in your heart brings in the heavyweight champion to take you the rest of the way.

Between you and God, you have this. You can do it. And each time you do, your joy, pride, and security in your pure identity will grow. Remember, too, that when you win a battle against a temptation, you'll grow strength to fight other temptations as well. Maybe you're working hard at a sport and there are days that the last thing you want to do is practice. As you show yourself that with God you can fight sexual temptation, you'll have the "I can do this" mindset to push through when you're tempted to slack off in practice. Same with losing weight or acing a class or going after some other major goal in your life—the more you show yourself strong in this area, the more you'll believe you can be strong in other areas too.

"One huge benefit to living a pure life is to say that I made a promise with God and I kept it."

~Alex

BENEFIT SIX: Other people will look up to you

You could feed all the children in Africa. You could serve at the Salvation Army every weekend. You could ace all your tests and obey your parents perfectly. You could give all your money to the poor and be kind to every person you meet.

No matter your history, you can choose to live out your pure identity.

Don't underestimate the power of your decisions to impact other lives. As you guard your thoughts, actions, and behavior, you are influencing untold people around you. As you turn the channel on the TV or change the radio station, as you stand for God and for his goodness, you are influencing everyone in your circle. You are showing them that your faith isn't just something you do on Sundays—you are living out the fact your faith impacts every single area of your life and you don't care if they know it.

"If you live purity, you reflect Jesus. Someone might ask you about your faith and why you do what you do—and you'll get to tell them."
~Desiree

Jena came from a family of seven. They were a church-going family, but it was hard for the church stuff to translate over into their everyday lives of school and work. But as she grew older, Jena fell more and more in love with God. She had made a decision to stay pure, and when her parents gave her a purity ring, she proudly displayed it. She determined that she was going to save herself, guard her heart, and go after her God with all that she had inside her.

Jena was the middle child in her family. She toiled

through her teen years and fought to live her faith. It wasn't easy and it wasn't always perfect, but she knew that she was loved and she lived that love to others. For her twenty-first birthday, her family held a surprise party for her. As part of the party, each family member and several of her friends shared how she had impacted their lives.

She was amazed to hear what her mother said:

"Jena, you inspire me. You have chosen a path and you've stuck with it. You went after God and just watching your passion has really been a faith-builder for your father and me. I know we taught you about Jesus, but you taught us by how you have lived him every day. I'm humbled and proud to be your mom."

Family member after family member, friend after friend, stood up and shared how Jena's choice to live a life of pure devotion to Jesus made a difference in their world.

People are watching. You can't fake a pure life. As you choose to guard your heart, mind, and actions—as you live your love for God—you have the chance to make a difference in every life around you. As you face your Savior, as you give and receive love in that relationship, it will be contagious to the hearts and lives that surround you.

And even if this is about second chances for you, even if you have walked a broken road in the past, what you do *from this point forward* can transform the lives around you as they watch you change right in front of their eyes. Live this love that you've been given. Live purity. Give it all you have, and watch the hearts around you turn to the very same Savior who rescued you.

> *Dear friends, I urge you, as foreigners and exiles, to abstain from sinful desires, which wage war*

against your soul. Live such good lives among the pagans that, though they accuse you of doing wrong, they may see your good deeds and glorify God on the day he visits us (1 Peter 2:11–12).

Religion that God our Father accepts as pure and faultless is this: to look after orphans and widows in their distress and to keep oneself from being polluted by the world (James 1:27).

BENEFIT SEVEN: Nothing gets in the way of seeing your God kisses

God is in your world. He loves you through those God kisses: sunrises, sunsets, friends, circumstances, nature, the Bible … he's everywhere. When you're making decisions that go against his ways, it can be tougher to see all the good things he's doing in your life. It's like when a little kid sticks his hand in the cookie jar and takes a whole bunch of extra cookies. He's got chocolate all over his lips and a cookie in each hand. His mom walks in with a gift and calls him over. But he's afraid. After all, what if Mom sees the cookies in his hand or the chocolate on his lips? So instead of running over to Mom, he hides behind the curtain—and he misses out on the sweet gift Mom was about to give him.

That's what happens when we do things that we know God doesn't want us to do. Just like a little kid, we tend to hide our face from him, and we miss out on seeing all the good gifts he has for us in a day.

Choosing well in this area keeps you from hiding behind the curtain in your relationship with God. That means you get to see and receive and enjoy all the God kisses your heart can hold.

Guarding your pure walk benefits dating relationships, your view of yourself, and your experiences with God—all for good. In the next chapter we'll talk about some practical tools to help you live purity in your dating relationships—from who to date to how to end an evening without smooching through your curfew. This doesn't mean that you need to run out and find a Romeo to practice with—if you aren't dating now, there's no hurry. In fact, some of you may not have any desire to date, and others may not be allowed to yet. That's all okay. Reading the tools in the next chapter will simply equip you if and when you are ready; and if dating is not in your future, those same tools will help you when it comes to helping your friends as they date.

For now, answer the discussion questions to remind yourself how choosing purity can strengthen your heart and your faith, and also influence any dating relationships for good.

DISCUSSION/JOURNAL QUESTIONS

Can you see how making pure choices would benefit a dating relationship? What benefit inspires you the most? Why?

Do you believe there are young men who value purity out there? Does that help you stand strong in your own convictions? Why or why not?

Are you willing to wait for a young man like Ben? If so, write a prayer in your journal or share a prayer as a group, asking God to help you in that desire.

Share a recent decision you made in line with purity—whether it was turning away from an image, a thought, or an action. How did you feel about making that decision? Can you see how making a series of good decisions can help you in your relationship with God? And in other areas of your life? Explain.

CHAPTER FOUR

WHEN THE GUY CALLS

A plan for your dating relationship

First things first:

I mentioned this at the end of the last chapter, but I have to say it again: you don't have to date. I know, I know. It's a crazy thought and a wild concept, but it's true. *You do not have to date.* Sure, every TV show, every romantic comedy, every Top 40 hit pretty much talks about dating. Friends ask about it, gossip thrives on it ... In today's world, dating is portrayed as simply another step in life that every person must take.

It's not true.

God may have called you to singleness. Your parents may have said no to dating during this time in your life. You may not have any interest in it ever ...

That's okay. Learning to live a pure life will strengthen you as a single person and a follower of Jesus. I've said it before and I'll say it again: living purity is a lot more than saying no to a guy who wants sex.

But if you *do* decide to date or if you know anyone else

who chooses to date, move forward with these tools in your pocket.

TOOL ONE: BE CHOOSY

Madison didn't even know Craig existed until Melanie told her about him. "He has such a crush on you," Melanie said.

"Really? Who is he?"

Melanie described him. "Tall, shaggy dark hair ... comes into the gym all the time when we're working out?"

Madison still couldn't picture him. "Well, point him out next time we're there."

That afternoon Melanie pointed Craig out. It immediately clicked. Oh yeah, *Craig*. He'd dated a girl Madison knew from volleyball and it hadn't gone well, but he *was* pretty cute. He looked over and smiled. She smiled back.

It wasn't long before they'd exchanged numbers and Craig was calling and texting. He wasn't necessarily anyone Madison would choose, but he was cute and he seemed to like her a lot.

That counts for something, doesn't it?

I was a lot like Madison. I loved the feeling of being pursued. Unfortunately, I often felt obligated when someone liked me. If they had a crush on me, I felt like I should like them back. Part of it was my pleasing nature; I didn't like the idea of turning anyone away. But the other part of it was that I didn't have a clear definition of what I wanted in a guy and what I should look for in a relationship. If a guy liked me and I liked him, and we got along decently well, we started dating.

Those relationships usually didn't work out for long.

I heard one person describe it this way. "I was like a

stick on the river. I'd just float down the river and whatever limb snagged me, that's where I stayed until the current
pulled me away."

Relationships are too important to let happenstance define them. To just randomly float from one person to the next
depending on whom you meet, who likes you, and who is in
your path ... will not turn out well. I can almost guarantee
that someone you "float" into will not have a similar heart
in the area of purity. So be choosy. Start by thinking through
what is important in a relationship, and the character traits
you would like to see in the guy you date.

When I first started thinking about what I truly wanted
in someone, I created a list of one hundred attributes. I'm not
kidding. It took up five pages. I went from liking anyone who
liked me, to creating a list that Jesus himself might have had
a tough time fulfilling. I showed the list to one guy friend
who read it and then looked at me with his eyebrows raised.
"You want all of this in one guy? Seriously?"

Fine. I rewrote it and narrowed the list. Then I began to
ask God for a man who matched my deepest desires. I also
asked him to make me the woman who would match my
future husband's dreams.

The wonderful thing is that after I married Brian, I ran
across that old list of one hundred things I was looking for
in a guy. The only thing Brian didn't have was an innate passion for ballroom dancing.

Score!

In other words, it's okay to be choosy. Make a list of the
traits you want in a guy and make a list of the kind of woman
you want to be. Make both lists part of your prayer time, and
let God work in the rest.

> **"Purity means living up to the standards of who you are, and who your loved ones see you to be."**
> ~*Anonymous*

WHAT KIND OF STUFF SHOULD I PUT ON THE LIST?

The number one thing you can put on your list is "A guy who loves Jesus, and is growing in his faith." I'm not talking about someone who simply professes to be a Christian, but trust me in this, you want a guy who loves Jesus. A guy who loves Jesus worries about what Jesus thinks and does things to please him. That means he will do his best to honor you in all that he does. He'll be careful in his conversation and in his actions, and his life will be on course to be one lived in purity, honor, and integrity.

Ultimately, that's the kind of guy you want to marry. A man like that will love you out of the overflow of his relationship with God. It's a beautiful thing. As you love God with all your heart, and as he does the same, you'll both love each other from that deep well of God-love. When you have that kind of love pouring into you, you love your spouse through the good and bad, through weird hair days and goofy temper tantrums. You'll see each other through it all because you won't love each other for what the other person *does*, you'll love each other out of the pure depth of a God who loves you—or you will on most days, anyway.

Other things on your list might include specifics that are important to you. If you love the outdoors, you might want to avoid someone who hates sunlight. Maybe you know God has called you to missions; then you want to write down "heart for missions" as one of your top ten. You might also put in things like "owns his mistakes" or "works hard." Figure out a top-ten list of non-negotiable traits. These would be things that you wouldn't waver on, no matter what, and once that list is final, stick with it.

THE BAD-BOY ALLURE

There's another big reason to have a list: to remind yourself to avoid the bad boy.

What is it about him? Why do so many women fight an attraction for the brooding guy with the mysterious past? Part of it is what we've seen play out on TV and in the movies since we were babies. It usually goes something like this: Good girl meets bad boy. Good girl gives her everything to the bad boy—heart, body, love. Bad boy falls head over heels in love with good girl. Good girl reforms bad boy from his bad boy ways. Good girl and (now) good boy live happily ever after.

It's hard to resist being the heroine who loves a bad guy toward goodness. It's appealing to be the one person who understands him, the one who will make the difference in his life, the one who will rescue him from his deep, brooding thoughts.

Can you tell I've fallen for the bad boy before?

Here's a hard truth, but it's real: You can't save him. Your love can't save him. He may say that you are the only good thing in his world. He might remind you that without you, his life is sheer darkness. But if he looks to you to fix him and your love to make him better, what will happen when that doesn't work? God is the only one who can save hurting people. The only one. So when your love doesn't work, when the light you provide begins to dim, your brooding man will turn to another source to find his healing: it might be another good girl, it might be alcohol or drugs. But in the end, it won't be you and your heart will break.

The best thing you can do when you meet a bad boy that tugs at your heart is to call on some godly guys in your world (brother, youth pastor, friend), and ask them to pour Jesus into the guy. If your bad boy is receptive and grows in his faith, you've given him the best gift you could ever give him. And if he turns away from that answer, you'll have given yourself the best gift by protecting your heart—and your purity.

> **"I feel that the biggest struggle in purity is finding some-one who is on the same page. You may find a nice guy, but that does not mean he believes in the same standards of purity that you do."**
> *~Amari*

TOOL TWO: MAKE IT CLEAR FROM THE START— CREATE A PLAN

So you meet a guy that seems to have your top ten guy traits. Not only does he have the top ten, he's working on the top twenty things you would ever want in a guy. He asks you out for pizza and a movie ... Now what?

"Do we have to talk about purity on the first date?" Shelly asked me. "It seems weird to talk about that stuff so soon."

She's right. You shouldn't talk about that stuff on your first date. Talk about it *before* the first date. Make sure you are on the same page and set strong physical boundaries early on. If you don't talk about it then, when would you approach it? Trust me, you won't be thinking clearly when he wraps his arms around you and goes in for the good-night kiss. You won't be set up for success if you wait until you're cuddling on the couch to watch a movie.

"But what if he looks at me like I'm weird and changes his mind about going out with me?" Shelly asked after I told her my idea.

"Well, if he looks at you weird or changes his mind, you'll know right off the bat that he was a whole lot more interested in your body than in your heart. And wouldn't you want to know right up front if he is the type of guy who is only interested in one thing?"

Be straightforward. Talk about your desire to live a pure life early on. Share how you love God and how you're guarding your heart, mind, and body from sexual images, thoughts, and touch.

A guy who truly does love Jesus will be glad you brought the pure life up. He will look in your earnest eyes and nod his agreement. He's trying to do the same thing, so you try to figure it out together: *What will be our game plan to help each other stay on track?*

See, loving Jesus and desiring to live his ways will not automatically protect you from the temptation to touch and explore each other. There are lots of godly kids who have made choices they regret simply because they didn't have a plan in place, or the tools to really make it happen.

"I wouldn't do anything with my boyfriend that I couldn't do in a public place. A kiss, holding hands, a little bit of cuddling—that's it."

~Kara

So, to help you get your relationship off to a good start, here are a few ideas you can introduce into your plan:

COMMIT TO PURITY IN ALL AREAS OF COMMUNICATION

Promise that you won't tempt each other with racy text messages, conversations, or banter. It's too easy to slide into deeper and more intimate waters. Pretty soon, images come to mind, and thoughts and storylines follow soon after. Remember, the body ultimately lives out what the mind is consumed with—commit to keeping your thoughts and communication above board.

SPEND TIME IN GROUPS

God wired our bodies to long for each other. He did that so our marriages would be all kinds of spicy and fun (we'll talk about that more later), so be smart: don't spend lots of time alone. You are not Superwoman. He is not Superman. The more time you spend in intimate surroundings (like a car, a living room, or a friend's house), the more you'll be tempted to turn that longing into a reality. When you date, go out in public. If you're worried about the car time after a date, meet him somewhere and drive home alone or get a ride with a friend or parent. If you begin your dating relationship with that boundary in place, you'll be much more likely to follow through and maintain it. Trying to back off on alone time together *after* you've crossed lines will be much harder. Be intentional right at the start and make sure to date in public.

INVITE ACCOUNTABILITY

"I wish I had someone to relate to, someone who could help me stay strong."
~Kayla

Jennifer called me after every date with Brian. Jennifer is my dear friend and accountability partner, and she was very protective of what God had been doing in my singleness. She didn't want any kind of guy stuff getting in the way, so Jennifer would call me up (she lived a few states away) and grill me about my time with Brian.

My favorite line went something like this: "Okay, Elsa. You have to be honest with me. Did he touch your boobies?"

I was like a little kid. Just hearing her say the word *booby* made me giggle. "Does it count if he brushed his elbow against them?" I'd ask.

She'd laugh. Every time.

"Yes, that counts!"

Oh my. I am so grateful for Jennifer. Knowing I had to answer that question did wonders to keep both Brian and me on the straight and narrow.

Brian had guys in his life too. Men who were protective of his faith journey and who wanted to make sure that he maintained his commitment to purity.

Accountability helps. Especially in the realm of dating, it's just good to know that people have your back. Whether they commit to praying for your dating relationship or they ask you the hard questions to help remind you of truth, having some friends in the battle will make a difference.

Trust me, it's easy to lose sight of God's purposes when

you're dating. It's hard to remember why you've been called to purity or why it's even worth it to fight the feelings that can sweep you away. You need your girlfriends to remind you of the truth. Otherwise, it's way too easy to start talking yourself into things that you never imagined you'd do.

THINK PROTECTION (OF EACH OTHER)

When Brian and I began dating, it helped me to think about protecting his faith journey. I had a lot of respect for his relationship with God and the last thing I wanted was to be the cause of him falling away from that connectedness. I wanted to bring out good things in him. Thinking about protecting his faith gave me the added fuel to stand firm when temptation crowded in.

Remind each other often that this is bigger than saying no to sex. It's about loving God, trusting that he has a best, and not letting anything else get in the way. Protect each other's faith and be vocal about it.

TOOL THREE: DON'T TAKE HIS DISTANCE PERSONALLY

Don't you like me?

Shonda stole a glance at Donovan as they sat in the movie theater. It was his eyes that caught her breath every time. And that smile. She loved that smile.

This was their third date and Shonda was hoping that tonight he would finally kiss her good night. She thought for sure he would kiss her the last two times they went out, but he'd only hugged her awkwardly before quickly walking away.

Some of Shonda's friends couldn't believe it. "You mean he hasn't kissed you yet? What's wrong with him?"

Shonda stole another glance at him. Maybe he just didn't like her very much. Or maybe he didn't like her *that way* at all.

Shonda thought to another conversation she'd had with her closest friend, Dierdre. "But didn't you tell him you wanted to stay totally pure in your relationship? What if he's just trying to respect that?"

Shonda considered it, but she just couldn't shake the doubt. He probably just wasn't very attracted to her. She sighed. *I knew it. This has all been too good to be true anyway.* Maybe tonight, if he didn't kiss her, she'd lean in to kiss him and see if he took the bait. That would definitely tell the tale.

Yup, that's what she'd do. Flush him out and see if he cared at all.

If we're honest, we'd all have to admit that sometimes purity can drive us crazy. We want guys to be pure and to honor our boundaries, but when they don't make some kind of move, we get offended. We think the worst: *He doesn't like me. He doesn't want me. I knew it.*

Whatever the thought may be, it's usually not, *Wow, what a nice guy. He's honoring the physical boundary we've set up.* We take his aloofness personally, and ultimately try to tempt him to cross a line to prove that he finds us attractive.

Talk about sending mixed messages!

Be aware of this: If you go into a dating relationship where the guy keeps some physical distance, don't take it personally. He's a young man doing his best to honor God and honor you. Give him a break and let him keep that distance. Shore up any insecurity and don't tempt him in order to feel better about yourself.

It makes sense that this would be an issue. So often we tie physical advances to emotional affection. But if a guy is fighting physical urges to honor your purity, he's communicating more emotional attraction than you may realize. He's fighting a huge fight within himself, and he's doing it for his God and for you. Let that encourage your heart and don't push him any further.

One young man put it this way: "I didn't mean to be mean or anything, I just had to leave quick. I was thinking about her, about kissing her, about doing other things … and I just had to get away. I know she thought I was rude, but I really was just trying to do the right thing."

This battle you're waging with your guy is no easy battle. Neither one of you will do it perfectly, so be careful not to take offense if he's doing what he can to keep his hands off you. Do your best to swallow your insecurities and take it as a compliment.

TOOL FOUR: DRESS TO ATTRACT, NOT TO TEMPT

Kelly knew she should stay out of that store, but she couldn't seem to help herself. It was the after-holiday sale and so many of their tops were a steal. Kelly went into the dressing room and tried on three different tops. All of the shirts were low-cut and she knew she was showing too much cleavage … but … *Honestly,* she thought as she checked herself out in the mirror, *I do look good!*

Kelly went to the register with the three tops in hand.

Later that evening, Kelly went to the movies with her boyfriend. She was wearing her new shirt and guys were checking her out as they walked by. Kelly knew her boyfriend was having a tough time keeping his eyes on her face as well—and she found herself relishing his struggle ... just a little. It felt good to be found so attractive, and every once in a while she'd catch the eyes of a guy passing by and smile. They'd always smile back.

She was flirting, but it wasn't a big deal.

Create in me a pure heart, O God, and renew a steadfast spirit within me.

Psalm 51:10

I get it. I know. I can remember walking with my brother on a beach boardwalk one time. I was wearing a sports bra with a light knit top over it. My knit top kept sliding off one shoulder and I remember the boys walking by, glancing over and letting their eyes drop. Their attention brought a sense of confidence and excitement—an adrenaline rush. My brother grabbed the edge of the knit top and pulled it back over my shoulder. He was a strong believer and I remember thinking, *What's the big deal? Gosh, he's so uptight ...* Now I think back and feel a sense of gratitude for my brother's kindness. He knew those guys weren't thinking, "Wow, she's beautiful and I bet she has a wonderful heart and a great mind to boot." No, their response was purely physical—with little care for anything beyond a quick physical rush.

See, I'd made the same mistake we just talked about. I made the assumption that a lingering look meant more than just a base physical attraction. Like somehow that lingering look would lead to a lingering conversation and an eventual lingering kiss and on to a lingering together for a lingering lifetime.

Whatever.

If I had really been thinking about it, I would have realized that we were all using each other that day. I was using the guys to feel good about myself. The guys were using me for a quick thrill. I would have also recognized that because a guy looked at me, he was probably looking at every other girl that walked by. His looking didn't make me special or give me value.

So why did I care so much if I caught a man's eye? Or feel so good if I was successful in tempting my boyfriend with my body? Why did that matter to me?

This is a big one. If this is an issue for you, you have to take some time to figure out why it's so important to tempt your guy or draw the gaze of guys that walk past. For me, I viewed myself based on how guys viewed me. If three guys looked at me as I walked down the street, that was a good day. If no one glanced my way, I felt ugly. If I tempted my boyfriend and caused him to struggle, he really loved me. If he didn't struggle that day, I must not have done my job or I must not look very pretty. Gauging my day and my sense of self by how many guys glanced my way was a dangerous place to live. If you're with me, if that's where you find your value, you know what I'm talking about. You know the temptation to dress more and more provocatively to draw their eyes.

Now, don't get me wrong. It's okay to want to look beautiful. It's okay to care about your appearance, and to enjoy fashion. That's normal and natural. It's also normal to want to draw the attention of a guy you care about. God put that desire inside of us. After all, we want our date to think we're beautiful, and in the marriage environment we're designed to draw our guy in and make him all crazy with our womanly ways. Where it gets dangerous is when we are *dependent* on the looks of men to define our beauty. It's dangerous when we expose our bodies to try to draw the attention of any and every guy we pass on the street. If that's what you spend a lot of time thinking about, there might be more going on underneath the surface. For me, I didn't feel very lovable on the inside, so using my body to draw a guy's glance was a way that I could feel good about myself. Maybe you have felt the same way. Maybe you think that your body is the only thing beautiful about you, so you depend on it to get something that feels like love.

Others of us like the power. We like to know that our bodies make a guy weak at the knees. We might dress that way for the simple reason of enjoying the sense of power that our sexuality brings.

No matter the reason, be real with our God about what you're feeling. Talk to a friend. Talk to a trusted adult. Ask God to show you why you might be making the decision to draw attention to your body. Is it solely about the power? Or is there a painful history underneath it all? A demeaning relationship in your past? A sense that you are somehow not enough? Whatever it is, I promise you that God longs to touch and heal and change that place. He did it with me, and I know he can do it with you. Not that you'll start dressing poorly or that guys won't be attracted to you—that's not the case at all. He just wants to deal with the place that is totally dependent on their reaction. He wants guys to be attracted for all the right reasons. See, God doesn't view you as a body only, and he wants you to know that you are so much more than your physical appearance.

In the meantime, dress modestly—not homely, but modestly. You can dress in fashion without showing off your boobs. Modesty doesn't mean baggy jeans and bulky sweaters, it just means being sensitive to how much skin you're exposing as you embrace your fashion sense. Also, put some time and thought into consciously avoiding the eyes of the guys you meet. In other words, try not to gauge your impact on them as you walk into the room. Instead, focus on other things, be intentional in talking to people you might not normally chat with ... If you are dating, ask your boyfriend if he feels like you've been overly provocative with him, making it tough on your mutual commitment to purity. Ask his forgiveness and commit to honoring him by not putting him in that position. Guys are wired to respond more to visual stimulus, so do your best to look out for him in that way.

In the last chapter, we talked about Ben and how he was willing to wait for you, asking you to wait for him (or a guy like him). We talked a lot about looking for a guy who is willing to seek after God with all his heart, put aside his own desires, and guard your purity. Now is your chance to do the same. Guard his purity. Ask for God's help and then set aside that need to be checked out ... do your best to put aside the insecurity or the hunger in honor of his journey.

This purity thing is a two-way street.

The goal of this command is love, which comes from a pure heart and a good conscience and a sincere faith.

1 Timothy 1:5

BOTTOM LINE

The best thing you can do to guard your purity and the purity of the guy you are dating is for both of you to stay connected to God. Be intentional in spending time with God and keep that your main focus.

For a long time, I did that all wrong. God was actually my rebound man. If I didn't have someone in my life, I would pay more attention to my faith. But the minute someone interesting entered my world, I tended to abandon my God and go after the arms I could feel and the eyes I could see. The more I fell into that relationship, the less I would pay attention to God.

And that's usually when things would start to fall apart. Without that close connection to God, I didn't have the desire or the willingness to guard my purity in the same way. I conveniently forgot that he had my best interest at heart and I would start going my own way, letting my desires take over.

When I finally learned from enough bad choices, I began dating with a whole different perspective. Never again would a guy take God's place. Never again would I walk away from my values for someone.

So hold close to the one who loves you most. Hold close and make sure he remains your first love. You want to be in a relationship where you feel wonderful connecting with God every day. If you find yourself hiding like the little kid with chocolate chip cookies we discussed earlier, do a heart check and see if this is the right relationship for you.

When you can spend time with someone and then go before God with a pure and joyful heart, you'll know you have a good thing.

Don't settle for anything less.

DISCUSSION/JOURNAL QUESTIONS

Have you ever created a list of the top ten attributes you would like in the man of your dreams? Write or share the top three things that matter most to you.

As you thought about what you want in a guy, what character traits do you think a man might want in a woman? What steps can you take to become the woman you want to be?

Are you dating now? Have you set healthy boundaries? If not, which of the tools that we discussed can you bring into your relationship today? Commit to making it happen.

Do you struggle with finding your value in the looks of guys? Be honest with yourself and God—think of one thing you can do to begin building your value in other ways.

CHAPTER FIVE

REALITY CHECK

The painful consequences when temptation gets the best of you

Saleeda was late—and she was scared to death. This was not good. *We were careful*, she thought to herself, *so how could this be happening?* She had a really bad feeling that this was not going to turn out well. *Oh, God, please don't let me be pregnant.* Just the thought of it made her stomach turn. *What if I am? How am I going to tell my parents? How am I going to tell Todd? Oh, God, please. I'm not ready for this. I can't do this. I'm only sixteen years old. Please …*

Janelle had no idea that oral sex could transmit a sexually transmitted disease. *How was I supposed to know? No one told us about that!* She felt so embarrassed and ashamed. She'd thought oral sex was a safe way to connect with a guy without actually having sex. The reality that now she had herpes, and would have it for the rest of her life … the thought made her sick to her stomach. *Oh, God, why did I even go there?*

Kandace couldn't get the images out of her brain. It was

like they were seared into her conscience and she couldn't erase them. It's not like she ever wanted to look at that stuff, but when her friends took her to that website, she couldn't tear her eyes away. Now the images seemed to be right there all the time. She'd be thinking about homework and they'd pop into her brain ... or she'd be right in the middle of a conversation and her thoughts would take her there. *Oh, God, I feel like I'm never going to be clean again ... I hate this feeling. Please, help me.*

Let's be real. We talked about the amazing benefits that come from choosing to live purely, but the harsh reality also remains—making poor choices will hurt you. Saleeda, Janelle, and Kandace experienced this firsthand, and it's likely you either know what they are feeling, or you know friends who have been in their exact situation.

> *It won't happen to me.* (That's what every girl thinks.)
>
> *My boyfriend doesn't have a sexually transmitted disease.*
>
> *I'm not going to get pregnant.*
>
> *That stuff won't get into my brain ...*

It's part of human nature. We think we're immune to the painful consequences that other people experience.

But we're not.

A CLOSER LOOK

As much as I would like to skip over this chapter, we're going to take a brief look at some of the consequences that can come as a result of bad choices in the area of purity. The more knowledge you have, the better equipped you'll be. Remember, God wants to protect you from harm. He wants to keep you from danger. If you've walked through some of these things already, we'll talk about second chances in the next chapter. But for now, let's take a closer look at some of the pits God wants you to avoid.

> **"If you choose purity in physical stuff, you don't have to worry about getting any STDs. You also don't have to worry about having a baby before you're ready. Overall, there is a lot less stress in dating when you stand firm on your commitment to be physically pure."**
> *~Emilie*

THE DANGERS OF SEX:

A BROKEN HEART

God meant for sex to be a physical and spiritual bond you share with one safe person for the rest of your life. If you have sex in a dating relationship, you're left completely open to deep pain. You've given your most vulnerable, naked self to that person ... and if that person eventually walks out of your life, how can your heart *not* be broken? How devastating to know that you gave everything and that it was somehow not enough. God wants to protect you from ever feeling used and discarded. Marriage (as God designed it) guards your heart. Sex outside of marriage breaks your heart—I can totally attest to that reality. God wants to protect you from a broken heart.

PREGNANCY

God meant for every child to have two loving parents who would stick around, together. Risking pregnancy outside of marriage is dangerous. You've probably heard it a hundred times, but abstinence is the only full-proof protection against bringing a child into this world. You're young; you still have some growing to do yourself. God wants to protect that process for you, to give you time to grow up and become the woman you were called to be. In a marriage relationship, you share the duties and responsibilities of raising that child. God never meant for you to have to go it alone—having sex while dating increases that risk.

BUT WHAT IF I AM PREGNANT?

If you are pregnant (or know of a friend who is pregnant), please know that God still cares for you (or her). He has not walked away and he can still see you through this. Please talk with your parents, and if they aren't safe people, talk with your youth pastor or a local Christian crisis pregnancy center first. Please choose life for your baby. Depending on your circumstances, you can opt to raise your child yourself, or you can put her into the arms of a loving couple who can't have children of their own. What an incredible gift you would offer.

Even as I write these words, I'm praying that God would open a door for you to walk through, and that you will find safe support wrapped in grace.

STDS

Most of us tend to think that good-looking, charming people can't possibly have an STD (sexually transmitted disease). *Not Mark*, we think. *Not Dalton, he's smart and very good-looking, he hasn't even had a lot of girlfriends.* But here's the truth: good looks, intelligence, and a charming personality do not guard against a sexually transmitted disease, and it only takes one sexual encounter for you to end up with one. An astounding 9.1 million teens and young adults ages fifteen to twenty-four contract an STD each year. And STDs are not pleasant: AIDS is a killer; gonorrhea and chlamydia may not have symptoms, and if left untreated can impact a woman's ability to have children; herpes doesn't ever go away; syphillis, in its latent stages, can cause paralysis, gradual blindness, and dementia—and ultimately death. No wonder God calls you to pure decisions prior to marriage and pure decisions within marriage! He wants to protect you in every way!

THE DANGERS OF GIVING YOUR HEART AWAY

I was a lovesick fool. Seriously, I fell in love way too much. I crossed lines physically when I was sixteen, but I opened the door to that decision by giving my heart away long before that. I kept a photo album of my favorite TV stars all throughout my middle school years—and I can promise you that it wasn't a compilation based on character traits. It was all about the good-looking guys that caught my eye—but oh, how I "loved" them! If anyone had questioned me, I would have poured out my true devotion. I'm embarrassed to even admit this, but I can remember kissing the TV screen when one particular studly guy came on—wow, did my brothers have a field day with that one! And it wasn't just TV personalities. When I had a crush on a guy, starting back in the third grade, I didn't just think about him once in a while. He would consume my thoughts. I'd talk about him to friends and family, doodle his name on my notebooks, talk to God about him: "God, I really like him. Please let him notice me …"

I spent so much time giving my heart away to anyone who captured my interest that giving my body away wasn't such a stretch.

You've heard it before: guard your heart. Don't run down the path toward marriage and forever-after when you're just getting to know someone. But what does guarding your heart really look like? For me, it began by talking to God in real ways. I said something like, "Lord, you know me. You know I'm prone to getting wrapped up in a guy. Will you please help me to recognize when I'm going off the deep end and teach me to reign it all in? Please hold on to my heart until it's the right time to give it away." God knows you best and loves you most, so he's the one best able to help you in this. After going to God, get some good people around you. Ask them to knock you silly if you start acting goofy over someone you just met. That someone in my life was Jennifer. She was the same one who would ask me the booby question. If I started obsessing over a guy or getting too caught up in a relationship, she had permission to talk to me straight and remind me that no guy was ever actually going to swing me up onto a horse and ride off into the sunset.

Then, as you talk to God and lean on friends, watch what you say to the guy you're interested in. Don't let yourself jump to the immediate "love" statement or any kind of proclamation of undying devotion. Save forever promises until your wedding day.

Remember, purity is keeping your heart safely in God's care. If you fall head over heels for every guy that draws your interest, you'll be much more likely to compromise your values to get into or stay in a relationship with him.

THE DANGERS OF ONLINE COMPROMISE:

CURIOSITY GONE WILD

I remember thumbing through a *National Geographic* to see what women's bodies looked like. I was so curious to see what my boobies would grow to become that at seven and eight years old, I was leafing through nature magazines to try to figure it out. I was curious. Unfortunately, curiosity today can lead to a lot more dangerous content than some half-naked tribal women. The dangers of pornography run deep. And it's not just curiosity that will land you there. One wrong letter tapped into a search engine or one click through a disguised link and you can find yourself looking at images that both intrigue and repulse you.

Before we go further, here's an important truth to remember: You are not wacky, weird, or broken if you find yourself curious about naked bodies. There is nothing wrong with you if the images intrigue you. You were wired to be drawn in and as a sexual being, you will want to see more. At the same time, you might feel repulsed and embarrassed—that's because you weren't meant to linger on nakedness outside of marriage. So don't be too hard on yourself if you find yourself drawn to online images, but at the same time, don't let

ELSA KOK COLOPY

the attraction cause you to give in to temptation. Curiosity unchecked can lead you to some dark places. What began as a quick "I just want to see ..." can lead to an addiction. What you once looked at won't satisfy in the same way, so you start looking at darker and more degrading images. Before you even realize it, you can find yourself totally consumed in your thought life, totally caught up in online stimulation, and completely disengaged from real-life relationships and the reality that there are warm, beautiful beating hearts tucked inside those naked bodies—hearts that God designed, hearts worthy of your respect and honor.

ANONYMOUS INTERACTION

You can be anyone you want to be online. You can have the hair of shampoo commercials, the body of a lingerie model, and the witty mind of a worldly, wild woman. Creating an online version of yourself can be very appealing. Online communities, gaming connections, and social networking make it a whole lot easier for us to create a braver, sexier, more attractive version of ourselves. It's an easy escape ... but is it really just an escape? Guard yourself, because this fake world can become a lot more appealing than the real one—and as it takes up more and more of your time, as you spend more and more of your heart in relationships with people you've never met face-to-face, it can actually steal you from the passion, purpose, and real-life relationship God has for you.

We'll talk more about navigating online and digital communication in chapter nine, but for now, know that what you look at and how you interact with others can become a quick pitfall into dark places. Guard your heart and your mind in online interactions.

THE DANGERS OF DABBLING IN FANTASIES

Thoughts lead to actions. Think of a recent craving. Maybe you craved chocolate or salty snacks or a milkshake. I remember craving cigarettes badly. I spent a long, long time smoking. Then I quit. I haven't had much desire to go back, but every once in a while I smell cigarette smoke, or I see someone smoking, and the desire will pop into my brain. I've learned now to quickly turn my thoughts to other things, but what I used to do was just park on that thought. *Boy, it would be nice to sit outside with a cup of coffee and smoke a cigarette. I could have just one and it wouldn't make a difference. It's just that it smells good, and really, what's the big deal?* Oh my goodness, I could talk myself into anything. But what happens when you really grab hold of a desire, roll it around on your tongue, imagine it happening, and then play out what it would feel like when it does? Forget it. You're done. In the Bible, the book of James tackles this by talking about how our desires give birth to sin. In other words, when you let your thoughts be consumed with what might be and what could happen, you head down a path where actions are sure to follow. If you struggle with your thoughts, you'll have to be really intentional about doing what Scripture calls *taking thoughts captive*. In other words, if you find yourself headed down a broken path in your mind, you literally have to grab that thought, imagine tossing it away, and then think of other things. Your thoughts won't change by occasionally wishing they would— you'll have to redirect them on purpose. The more you do that, the more you'll be the one in charge, as opposed to allowing your thoughts and fantasies to lead your body into action.

THE BIGGEST LOSS OF ALL

The biggest loss when you choose to dabble in sex, online compromise, and dangerous thinking is that you take your eyes off your first love. See if this scenario can help you take this truth to the heart level:

Think of the person that you love most in the world. Maybe it's your mom or dad, your boyfriend, your little brother or sister, or even your best friend. Imagine you are standing face-to-face with that person. Picture their eyes, their smile, the silly way they laugh. Do you have it? The image is clear? Okay, so you know that your loved one is safest with you. You love him or her with a pure heart. Then out of the corner of your eye, you see someone approaching. He is smiling, but you know there's something sinister beneath his grin. He comes to the two of you and is able to distract your loved one from your gaze. He's laughing, pointing to something in the distance. You do your best to hold your loved one's eyes. You reach out your hand, but you are brushed aside. Your loved one turns away, distracted, and begins to wander off with this stranger, this person who harbors only evil in his heart.

Your heart is breaking. *No, please. Don't go.*

Your loved one seems oblivious to your cries.

You know he or she is headed to a dark place, but you feel helpless.

Pause here. Feel that longing in your heart. Feel the depth of wanting to protect the one you love. That is what our God feels. You are his beloved. You are safest with him.

He loves you with a pure heart. He adores your eyes, the tilt of your chin, the way you laugh that deep belly laugh with your friends. He sees your future and it looks so beautiful. He's excited for a lifetime of relationship with you and he can't wait to take you on adventures under his care. He delights in your desire to know him and he can't wait to show you the world through his eyes. He has so much for you, there in his presence. He believes in you, cares for you, will fight for you and guard you—in mind, body, and spirit.

But he is also a gentleman.

If you choose to walk away, he will let you go. If you brush him aside, he will stand, tears in his eyes, and watch you leave. He will never force you to stay. Love doesn't do that.

And that smirking stranger? He is the enemy who wants to distract you from God's gaze. He wants you to get lost in images on a computer screen, he wants you to get completely wrapped up in a sexual relationship with your boyfriend so that you lose sight of God and lose sight of the love he has for you. This enemy wants to consume you with things that make you feel dirty so that you don't turn to God. His victory comes when you walk away from the good things God has for you, the plans of the one who loves you most.

Sin is crouching at your door; it desires to have you, but you must rule over it.

Genesis 4:7

The thief comes only to steal and kill and destroy; I have come that they may have life, and have it to the full.

John 10:10

Don't go. Don't leave your loving, passionate, valiant God. You are safest when your eyes stay fixed on him. Living purity is saying yes to that kind of love. It's staying in the safety of your God's gaze. Anything that distracts you from that relationship is something you want to keep out of your life.

If you've struggled in this area, you know what I'm talking about. You know the feeling of loss and sadness. You know the moments you turned your head and willingly walked away. You've felt that sinking feeling even as you kept walking.

As much as it's in your ability to control, don't walk away. Don't let it happen. Choose God. Choose love. Choose the one who knows you best and loves you most.

You will never regret that choice.

DISCUSSION/JOURNAL QUESTIONS

Have you experienced any of the consequences described in this chapter? Share what it meant to walk through that experience.

If you had a close friend dabbling in things that will harm her (pornography or premarital sex) what would you say to her? Can you take that same counsel for yourself? Why or why not?

Are you able to picture God as a loving gentleman who longs to protect you from harmful influences? Why or why not?

Take a moment to write a prayer to God, asking him to help you put him first. Sit quietly afterward. See what God might whisper to your heart in return.

CHAPTER SIX

SECOND CHANCES

When you feel like all is lost, God can make things right

"How can I regain my purity if I feel like I've lost it over something small and almost insignificant?"
~Wynter

We all need second chances.

Not a single one of us gets through this life with a perfect track record. Whether you've struggled in the area of purity or you've struggled in other areas, we all need grace. Thankfully, that's the beauty of being in relationship with a loving God. He is the giver of second chances, the one who can help us when we mess up, the one who can get us back on track again. He's also the one who can help when we've been hurt by other people. If you've been pushed in the area of purity, if someone has touched you or violated you, God is right there with you and he will walk every step of the road to healing with you.

Let's start by touching on the mistakes we make, and a little later in the chapter we'll talk about how to deal with it if someone has hurt you in this area.

Who can say, "I have kept my heart pure; I am clean and without sin"?

Proverbs 20:9

THE SLIPPERY SLOPE—YOUR OWN CHOICES

"There are so many times that we push down that sick-to-our-stomach feeling when we should listen to it instead."
~Hannah

Lori felt so ashamed. She never expected to be in this place. All the warnings she'd heard from her parents and youth group leaders seemed to echo in her brain. *Too late now*, she thought. Despair flooded her heart as the tears came ... *What have I done? I should have never had that drink.* At the time it seemed so harmless. She felt grown-up ... cool. She'd only have one, she promised herself.

But then one led to another, and pretty soon she wasn't thinking very clearly. Alex came over and sat beside her. All other thoughts scattered. Lori didn't expect Alex to put his arm around her, but when he did, she liked it. She didn't expect Alex to kiss her either, but then he did that too.

Lori replayed the rest of the evening in her brain and couldn't believe she'd really let things get so carried away. All those years of holding on to her purity, all those years of following the rules, and in one single evening, she felt like all was lost.

What's the point now? she thought.

She jumped in the shower and tried to scrub off every hint of Alex's cologne. She wondered if he was thinking of her, if he realized she'd never done any of those things before …

Kiara couldn't tear her eyes from the computer screen. She was repulsed and drawn in all at the same time. She couldn't seem to turn away even as everything in her called out to stop looking. *It's not right, this isn't right.*

Later that evening she felt embarrassed, worried that someone would discover her online exploration. But at the same time, she felt a pull to return. She shook her head; she wasn't that kind of girl … was she?

Maria stared at the words on her phone. They made her heart beat quicker and her face flush with warmth. Guys had flirted with her before, but never like this, never with these kinds of words. She wanted to tell him to go away, she wanted to ignore the message, but she really liked him. What was the big deal with a little flirting anyway? Her fingers hovered over the keys. *It's not like we're actually doing anything*, she thought. And began to type.

So exciting—the pull, the draw, the temptation to cross little lines to see what it might be like. And then one decision leads to another and suddenly you're wondering how things got so dark so fast.

You are not alone.

If you have experienced any of these things, it's important to realize that small compromises tend to lead to bigger ones.

Bigger compromises lead to heart-wrenching pain and severe consequences that can sideline you for years. Think about it: An innocent evening of making out can lead to passionate touch and ultimately sex. While you would have never planned to be pregnant or stuck with AIDS, a small compromise can start you down that path. Same with pornography. Stumbling accidentally onto images that draw you in is one thing, but if you're not diligent in protecting yourself, you could end up choosing to click through to more dramatic visuals. We don't ever think that we'll be the type of person to make those decisions, but it's easy to get lost in the feelings. Sexual temptation is so intense because it *does* feel so good. Everything in our bodies reacts and we want the feeling back again and again ...

In the face of those very real temptations, remind yourself of the loving God who wants to fight for you and protect you, and also remember that you have an enemy who wants to steal every good thing from you. And that enemy is brilliant. He lures you in with small choices, and once you start exposing your heart and mind to unhealthy things, he tempts you to cross the next line and the next. He's relentless in his desire to rob your sense of purity, because he knows that if he can do that, then he can flood you with shame. Shame is the feeling that you are somehow too broken, too tarnished, too far from God to ever be able to find your way back. It's a powerful feeling that can keep you from looking to God and feeling the life-changing love he has for you.

The enemy is a robber, a thief, seeking to kill and destroy. But he's not going to do that in one fell swoop. He's not going to saunter up and say, "Hey, Jennifer, how about you give yourself away to that guy over there and then feel bad for a lot of years, and then maybe drink to cover up those bad feelings and then, uh, we'll just call it good?"

You'd smack him or laugh in his face. "Whatever. I'm not ever going to do that."

He's the enemy. He's smart. He's going to sideline you by trying to get you to compromise in the little things.

Have a drink and feel grown-up.

Flirt. Go on, girl, what's the harm?

Look at that picture …

Step by step by step, until you find yourself deeper and more lost than you ever, ever wanted to be.

> **"I regret having sex the first time, because I care so much for the guy I'm with now—I wish I had waited."**
> *~Casey*

THE FIRST STEP

Does any of this sound familiar? Can you see areas in your life where you have compromised or where the enemy has gotten the best of you? If so, now is the time to run to your God, to call out and let his grace help you.

What does that look like in your day-to-day life? Here's how it begins:

FESS UP

Fessing up means that we agree with God that we messed up. We admit that we made a bad decision and we bring it to him. Unfortunately, a lot of us like to explain away the things we do. We'll gloss over a bad feeling or explain away our guilty conscience. Think of the things you've told yourself, or the things you've heard from your friends. See if any of these sound familiar:

> *I really like this guy. I feel differently than I have in any other relationship. I want to be close to him ... Is that so bad?*

> *Maybe I'm talking a little dirty, but at least I'm not out there doing it.*

> *Everybody watches that show. It's not a big deal. It's not like it gets in my brain or anything. It doesn't affect me.*

> *I'm not hurting anyone. So what if I check out a few things online?*

> *So I let my thoughts wander a little bit. Doesn't everyone?*

> *We're getting married anyway, so it's not like I'm sleeping around—we really love each other and we're going to be together forever.*

The first step toward a clean slate is being real about where you are, and admitting the truth to God. Tell him what you're thinking and feeling, even if you're feeling stubborn about admitting the bad choice. For me, my boyfriend was so important to me that I didn't really want to admit I was wrong. I would have been the one to say, "We're getting married anyway, so it's not like I'm sleeping around ..." Besides, I hadn't experienced any of the downside of having sex with my boyfriend. I knew I was supposed to feel sad about it, but I just didn't. At least early on.

I understand if you're in that place too. Tell God exactly

where you are and let him meet you there. For me, it would have sounded something like this: "God, I really love him. I know you wanted me to wait, but it felt so right that it's hard to feel badly about it. I know in my head that I was wrong, but in my heart I'm having a tough time seeing it. I need you. Please help me to feel your heart in all of this. I need your strength and understanding because otherwise it's just another rule that I want to break. I *do* want to follow you. I *want* to want you more than anything or anyone else—so please teach me your ways and help me to live them out. Please give me your passion and your strength to do that well."

God honors authentic prayers. He honors when people are real with him … he already knows if you're feeling stubborn and holding on to a bad choice with both hands, so you might as well tell him the truth and ask him to do the changing.

For others of you, you've faced the rough consequences and you're ready to give it up and set it at God's feet. Trust me, he's ready to take it. He wants to take the sadness, the pain, the guilt. He wants you to be able to leave your hurt at his feet and make different choices from this point forward. Tell him. Be real. He will forgive you. He never turns away a broken heart that is longing for relief. He never turns away from someone who trusts him enough to bring him her stuff. Now if you're pretty far into the relationship or addiction, you might need help letting go—whether it's a relationship, pornography, online connections—and you'll need God and his people to get you out. But your first step is here: talk to God and ask his forgiveness. He is more than able to meet you.

Let us draw near to God with a sincere heart and with the full assurance that faith brings, having our hearts sprinkled to cleanse us from a guilty conscience and having our bodies washed with pure water.

Hebrews 10:22

RECEIVE SCANDALOUS GRACE

"It's possible to regain purity, because if you really want to change your ways and ask God for forgiveness, he will forgive you and help you."

~Makenzie

"I don't know," Jenna told me. "It doesn't seem right. It seems like if you offer forgiveness like that, people will just take advantage of it. Girls will just do whatever they want with their boyfriends or whatever—and then they'll ask for God's forgiveness like it's no big deal. That just doesn't seem fair."

It's true. God's grace doesn't make sense. In fact, it *is* scandalous and amazing. It doesn't make sense. You get a clean slate and receive forgiveness no matter where you've been. As you come to God sorry over what you've done, he forgives you. And yes, in the face of such amazing grace, it could be tempting to think, *Ah, God will forgive me, so what does it really matter? Why deny myself in this moment if God will forgive me later?*

Again, be real with God in this. Just like it's good to be real if you find yourself wanting to hold on to a relationship or addiction with both hands, be real with God if you find yourself thinking this way about his forgiveness. Because what lies underneath that thought? When I did what I wanted in hopes that God would forgive me later, my motives looked something like this: *This feels so good it's worth whatever punishment God might hand out later.* Or *I'm in love and it really isn't a big deal anyway …* or *I want this and I don't want anyone else to tell me what to do. Even God.*

But my thinking didn't really fit. If God has a best for me in calling me to purity, then when I made bad decisions with my body, thoughts, or time, wasn't I just hurting myself? I totally didn't get that God was protecting me from hurt. The very fact that I wanted to lean on God's forgiveness tells me that I didn't realize how much purity mattered, or how much God loved me as he asked me to live it out.

It's like a little kid walking with her mom. Imagine a two-year-old whose mom is holding her hand as they cross the street. The little girl wants to run. She doesn't see a thing wrong with running and she can't understand why Mom is holding her hand. "Let me go!" she yells as she pulls and runs. But there are cars and semis coming down the street … Now that little girl could think like we do sometimes. *Mom will forgive me, I mean, she loves me, so of course she'll forgive me—so I'm going to run!* But that little girl isn't thinking about the right things. If she knew the reality of the situation, she would stay close and listen to her mom. She'd know that Mom is protecting her—and that while running itself isn't a bad thing, running in the street is very dangerous.

See the correlation? Yes, God will forgive you when you choose against his ways, but you are the one that will get run over—by a sexually transmitted disease, addiction to pornography, a broken heart. And he wants to protect you. It's important to know that sexuality and exploring your sexuality

d thing, but exploring it in ways outside of God's
_ _ ttle like running in the street. Very dangerous.

So if you find yourself in the place of hoping God will
forgive you later, talk to him. Ask for his forgiveness for that
deeper issue of not trusting his love, and ask him to teach
you his ways. For a long time I had this prayer on my mirror
in the bathroom:

> Teach me your way, LORD,
> that I may rely on your faithfulness;
> Give me an undivided heart,
> that I may fear your name.
> I will praise you, Lord my God, with all my
> heart;
> I will glorify your name forever.
> For great is your love toward me.
>
> Psalm 86:11–13

I knew that my heart was divided. I wanted to do my own
thing and I wanted God. I wanted my own way and I wanted
God's way. So I asked God to give me an undivided heart
so I wouldn't keep doubting him and running out into the
street. It really wasn't anything I could change on my own. I
needed God's help. I also needed his people—but we'll talk
about that in just a little bit.

For now, no matter where you are in this journey, run
to your God and fess up. If you've been stubborn and held
on with both hands, if you've made a bad choice with the
thought "God will forgive me later," if you've let yourself get
lost in thoughts, storylines, or computer images, or if you've
engaged in (willing) physical intimacy in any form, your

first step is to return to the one who loves you most. Run, walk, or crawl back to his loving arms.

"My biggest struggle in living purity is my past. After making all the mistakes, it becomes a whole lot harder to avoid making them again. The Devil knows what to use against me, but it's my faith in God and my purity that keep me strong against him."
~Bethany

Run. Walk. Crawl. He is waiting. There is an enemy in your life that would have you believe that if you've sinned, you shouldn't go back. If you've walked away, it's done—that you'll just keeping making the same mistakes over and over. It's not true. Run back to your God. I don't care if you've crossed one line or a thousand. Run to your God. Run to his embrace.

Remember as you bring your broken choice to him, he's already reaching to meet you. He picks you up, dusts you off, and holds you close. He takes away the burden of guilt and brings strength to face the temptations that will come.

For the grace of God has appeared that offers salvation to all people. It teaches us to say "No" to ungodliness and worldly passions, and to live self-controlled, upright and godly lives in this present age, while we wait for the blessed hope—the appearing of the glory of our great God and Savior, Jesus Christ, who gave himself for us to redeem us from all wickedness and to purify for himself a people that are his very own, eager to do what is good.

Titus 2:11–14

FESS UP TO A FRIEND

Once you own the choice and ask God for forgiveness, it's time to talk to someone you trust—and who is trustworthy. In James 5:16, it says, "Therefore confess your sins to each other and pray for each other so that you may be healed." That doesn't mean gathering some girls in the locker room and filling them in on your latest bad move. I made that mistake a few times—sharing way too much information in the totally wrong setting. The kind of sharing I'm talking about is done with someone who is a little further down the road in her faith journey. Maybe she's a friend from youth group, a youth pastor, a godly lady in the church. Ask if you can get together with her and then as you build the relationship, share your story.

I believe that God wants us to share our lives like that because we get to know what it's like to be known and loved, just as we are. Secrets are horrible. They suck the joy right out of life. But if you confess your secrets to someone who cares about you and that person still looks at you with a smile, loves you, and willingly prays for you, then suddenly you begin to think that there's hope after pain, and good choices that can come after bad. Then with your head held a little higher, you go on to live the life you were called to live, strengthened in ways you can't even explain.

RUN THE OTHER WAY

So you fess up to God and soak up his grace. Then you fess up to a good friend. *And then you stop making the same choice.* You quit texting the guy who wants to talk dirty. You put protective software on your computer. You have a conversation with the person you're dating and you refuse to spend time alone with him. You do whatever it takes (and a lot of the tools are in this book) to hold on to this new you and move forward in purity.

And that's the hard part, isn't it? It can be freeing and invigorating and totally inspiring to start fresh, to feel good about where you are, and to move forward with a smile. But what's usually the first thing that happens after you bring your heart to God and get a clean slate?

Big temptation comes.

And what if you fail that temptation ... or you stand firm for a while but then slip up in another area? Sometimes it can get so discouraging to try to live the perfectly pure life that you might want to throw in the towel completely.

Please don't. The key is to keep a short account. In other words, if you slip up, go through the process we just talked about—and quick. Fess up to God and to a friend, and then run the other way. Over time your strength will grow and grow. Old temptations won't sway you in the same way. Confidence will grow, and with each passing day you will become that stronger, more self-controlled, and godly person you were meant to be.

WHEN PURITY IS TRAMPLED

Frankie hated hearing about purity. Every time someone in the youth group or on the radio took on the topic, she felt sick to her stomach. She'd flash back to that day, two years and three weeks ago, when someone she didn't know took what didn't belong to him. She was raped. Now, not only did Frankie have the scars of being victimized, she also felt anything but pure.

Frankie isn't alone. Many of you reading these words know exactly what I'm talking about. Others of you have been touched inappropriately, pushed to compromise your values, or spoken to in demeaning ways.

If you're reading this and you *haven't* experienced these things, please keep reading. Someone may need you to help them sort through their feelings. This is a huge issue in the lives of young women today, so let's tackle it together.

> **"My biggest struggle is people with different values trying to pressure me to do something different."**
> *~Anonymous*

FIRST THINGS FIRST

This is not your fault. If you have been pushed, dishonored, or violated in any way, it is not your fault. You didn't deserve it, *period*. I don't care what thoughts might be racing through your brain right now:

> *Yeah, but I led him on …*
>
> *I shouldn't have been walking alone in the dark.*
>
> *I knew I shouldn't flirt with him, but I did it anyway.*
>
> *My friends told me I shouldn't be alone with him.*
>
> *I wore that outfit and I know it was a little much …*

Here is the truth: if you are struggling with guilt regarding what someone else did to you, please ask God to take it from you. Set it at his feet. *It is not your fault.* If you told someone no and they didn't honor what you asked, that is not your fault. You deserve respect, honor, and care. Please know that you did not deserve it and that what happened to you was wrong.

"My biggest struggle is that boys keep asking me to do things and I keep trying to say no."
~Anna

SO NOW WHAT?

Whatever your experience—whether you were violated by a friend, a relative, or a stranger—you have to tell someone. Talk to a trusted adult, preferably a female. Choose someone who has her head on straight and loves you. Let her know what happened and let her love you through the sadness. It *is* sad. It *is* heartbreaking and demeaning and painful. This isn't something you should brush off. Face it, talk with someone, and know that it's okay to feel sad about this loss. That trusted friend can help you walk through the emotions. For those of you who experienced violence or rape, I'm so very sorry. I wish I had the ability to sweep in and wipe away the memory, the pain, and the heartache. What happened to you is horrible, and you have every right to feel angry, sad, and betrayed. If only there were an easy way to get to the other side of the hurt, but there just isn't. As a result, you need someone to be with you through it all. Please talk with your parents, a pastor, or a good counselor. You'll need Jesus with skin on to remind you of how beautiful you are as you get rid of the things that feel ugly inside.

THE NATURAL QUESTIONS

Why, God? The questions bubble up in frustration and anger. *If God loves me and wanted to guard my purity, why would he allow someone to trample all over it? Why would a good God allow such a thing to happen?*

There is no easy answer to that. We live in a broken world with people who have chosen against God in horrific ways. Evil is a part of our world. Bad things happen that we can't explain or make sense of ...

A few years ago I lost my dad in a sailing accident. He went out for his normal sail and fell off of his boat, while the boat kept going and left him behind. My dad drowned that day and the Coast Guard found his body four miles out in the ocean. We were shocked and heartbroken. My whole family gathered together to say their good-byes, holding each other and crying as my mom scattered his ashes into the water he loved so much.

Such a huge sudden loss ... *Why God?*

Just twelve days later, the unthinkable happened again. My nephew Caleb, who had just been with us for my father's funeral, fell asleep at the wheel on the way home from a church event. It was late and he was tired—his car hit a tree and he was killed instantly.

He was only seventeen years old.

Our family was devastated. We didn't even have time to catch our breath from losing my dad before we had to say good-bye to Caleb. I can remember getting home after the two funerals and journaling my anger and sadness to God.

"Why, God? We pray for each other. We prayed for my dad, we prayed for Caleb's life for the last seventeen years. God, do you even hear our prayers?"

Less than an hour later, I received a text message from my brother. "Elsa, just thinking about you. I wanted you to know that God hears the cries of the hurting. He's with you, girl."

Sitting in church a few hours later, the pastor stopped in the middle of his message about something completely different from sorrow and said, "Do you know something? God loved the Israelites. And when they called out, when they were hurting and they called out, God heard their prayers."

Later in the afternoon, I got an email. "I was just thinking of you, Elsa. Just wanted you to know that God bends his ear to his children."

Three times. Three times in a row God let me know that he hears our prayers. He didn't answer my "Why" question, and we may never know (while we're on this planet) why bad things happen. But we can know beyond a shadow of a doubt that the God of the universe hears our prayers. He is deeply moved by our hurts and not a single tear goes unnoticed.

Another reality we can trust is that God *will* right every wrong. He is just and he is mighty. If we've been hurt by someone else, our fierce and holy God will bring justice (see Romans 12:19). In the meantime, he is working out consequences for that person. Whether it's time in prison, broken relationships, or painful circumstances, God is working even today to bring justice on your behalf.

Please know this: God isn't going anywhere. What happened to you was horrible, and he knows that it's going to take some time for you to see any kind of light at the end of this dark tunnel. Just know that there *is* light. Healing will come. The pain will lessen over time. And purity, this pure life that we've been talking about, can still be yours. With God's help and the love of good friends, you can know what it's like to feel safe in relationship again, and to love someone without fear of being hurt. It is possible to get through this trauma and reclaim who you are, piece by piece. There is hope.

As you grow in that, as you cry out to God, as you trust him to be your avenger and as you experience healing and see some light in your future, God will press it on your heart to forgive the offender. I can almost hear your reply. *What? Are you kidding?* But as difficult a request as it is, he doesn't ask you because he is not a just God, or because he isn't going to work out consequences in the life of the one who harmed you, but because forgiveness will free *you*. Lack of forgiveness builds a wall of bitterness in your heart and then the perpetrator will not only have violated you once, but he will violate you for years after by keeping you from knowing joy, peace, life, and healthy relationships. And remember, forgiveness is not saying what was done to you was okay, and it is not reentering a relationship with the person you forgive. Forgiveness is freeing that person from the debt they owe you. But always remember, they are still fully accountable to the courts, to earthly consequences and to our mighty, holy, and protective God for their actions.

Forgiveness is part of the process, but I want you to know that I am not minimizing what you've walked through or trying to sound ultra spiritual in the face of deep pain. Again, forgiveness frees *you*. This is another area where a trusted friend or counselor can help you. They can help you understand what forgiveness is, and what it isn't. They'll help you walk through the process and be your strength, so that you can forever leave this injustice in your past, so that you can grab hold of God's goodness and live forward with

deep passion and hope-filled joy. It is possible. It is
It is the nature of our God.

STAY CLOSE TO OUR GOD

Finally, all throughout the process of dealing with this heartache—from the initial shock and shame to the grief, anger,
and ultimately forgiveness—talk to our God. Call out to your
Savior. Let him know where you are, what you're feeling,
and how you're struggling. Be real. His shoulders are broad
enough for your anger. His heart is tender enough to meet
you in your sadness. He is not going anywhere as you wrestle through these things. He will be there. Ask him for special glimpses of his love and care. Ask him to bring healthy,
strong, and wise people into your life. Ask him to rebuild
your heart and restore your sense of purity.

He is good. He is trustworthy. He is mighty. He is crazy
about you. Reach out to him and hold on to his love.

THE GREATEST TRUTH

> **"I want to know when you are considered no longer
> pure, and how to date guys without feeling like you're
> somehow not good enough now."**
> *~Jordan*

Okay, I have something big to tell you, a truth that will give
you all you need to move forward with your head held high.
You are *pure*. No matter where you've been, what you've
done, or what has been done to you, your *core identity* is
pure. This is the beauty of what Jesus did for us on the cross.

If you have accepted Jesus Christ as your Lord and Savior, that means he gave you his purity. His righteousness became yours. He paid a tremendous price for you to have his identity, but it's a price he paid out of profound love. He fought for you like no man ever has or will and his pure identity is now yours. (Check out Isaiah 61:10, below.) Do you know what that means? It means that every day from this point forward, as you make choices toward purity, you are living out of who you *are* and who you *will always be*. Every time you slip up or choose poorly, run to God and he will scrub the stains from you and restore your purity again.

> **"Purity is created in the heart. It is a work of God within. Our behaviors and choices can be sin, but just as with any other sin, the blood of Christ covers over it. His redemption is thorough and it is complete; yes, even for those who feel impure. I encourage each to pursue purity, but to remember that purity is God-given. Purity is a condition of the heart after entering a relationship with Christ. We can neither obtain it or lose it by our behavior."**
> *~Carrie*

No one can take your purity. You can't give it away. Pure is who you are. The rest of this book will equip you to live your identity: a pure, lovely young woman—daughter of our King—a pure and beautiful bride.

I delight greatly in the LORD; my soul rejoices in my God. For he has clothed me with garments of salvation and arrayed me in a robe of his righteousness, as a

> *bridegroom adorns his head like a priest, and as a bride*
> *adorns herself with her jewels.*
>
> Isaiah 61:10

We've talked about how to navigate poor choices and how to work through the pain you've experienced. Now, in the coming chapter, let's talk about the daily battles you face and how to win every one.

Read on to find out more, but first, dive into the discussion/journal questions.

DISCUSSION/JOURNAL QUESTIONS

Have you made a choice to compromise your purity? Where are you with that decision? Are you feeling a little stubborn, wanting to hold on to it? Or are you ready to let it go? Either way, what is one step you can take to walk away from that choice?

If you have had your purity violated (no matter if that violation feels insignificant in light of others'), have you talked with anyone about it? Would you be willing to open your heart and walk through the emotions you've experienced?

Is there something in particular that keeps you from taking steps toward healing? Be honest.

Are you able to think of yourself as a pure young woman? That your purity is your identity and not simply based on choices? If not, ask God to help you make that adjustment in your thinking. Write a prayer in your journal or pray together as a small group.

CHAPTER SEVEN

THE WORLD WE LIVE IN

How to fight the big battles

You are a pure warrior, fighting the good fight of faith. You know the heart of your God and his love, you know the benefits of a pure life, and in the last chapter you learned how to ask God for a second chance or experience his healing if you've been hurt by another person.

So you're ready, armed with love and knowledge. But as any good warrior knows, understanding what you're fighting against is the key to helping you win the battles that lie ahead. You have to know the external and internal pressures that will push against your pure identity. What is the culture saying? What are your deepest desires and how are they defining your decisions? What about the church and others who profess to be Christians; how do they play into the fight?

Let's take a look at the battles that lie ahead and the truth you'll need to win each one.

WHAT OUR CULTURE SAYS

"My biggest struggle is feeling like the odd one out. I haven't had sex, but mostly everyone around me has ..."
~*Anonymous*

They looked at Brian with wide eyes. "You mean you're not going to sleep with her before you get married? Seriously?" They were shocked that my husband was choosing to wait until marriage. "What if things don't work out in that area? Don't you want to try things out? Make sure you're physically compatible?"

"Well," Brian said with a smile, "if I can't trust God for something like that, what can I trust him for? He wired us. He created us. If we fit, that's his gift. If on the far-out chance we have any issues, don't you think he can work in that too?"

"You're crazy."

"Not worth the risk, man."

Brian heard it, I heard it, and you'll probably hear it too. Waiting until marriage to pursue physical intimacy is nearly unheard of, and in our culture, you'll find yourself waging a battle as you go against the grain.

It's interesting that sexuality is one area where God's will and our culture are at complete odds. It's not like other things. Most authority figures, whether they believe in Jesus or not, will discourage you from trying out drugs. They'll stand against drinking or stealing or lying your way through school. They won't push you to skip classes, betray your friends, or speed in your car. But when it comes to sex or pornography, those things are winked at, allowed, and sometimes even encouraged. (*Especially* when it comes to guys.) Most teen and adult TV shows include premarital sex or a teenage boy tucking a magazine under his mattress. Popular books and movies picture teens groping each other in the theater, in the car, or behind the bleachers at school. Sexual prowess is glamorized and the sexier the outfit, the better.

It's no wonder that it's so easy to get sucked in! If the

message you receive is that desire should translate into action, then what are you supposed to do when desire comes your way? If you're told through TV shows and the media that teenagers are going wild, what will you do when the temptation to go wild hits your heart? And if pornography and premarital sex are portrayed as not only natural, but cool, how will you have the stamina to turn away?

Truth. That's the key to turning away from everything the culture tells you about purity. Because as you think about what the culture endorses, think about what happens in the real world as a result of those choices:

> Sex is portrayed as glamorous, but when a teenager gets pregnant, she's looked down upon.

> Pornography is winked at and condoned, but most sexual predators have a long history of pornography. Turns out looking isn't such an innocent pastime after all.

> Girls are taught to use their body and to dress seductively, only to find that men then see them as only sexual beings. They begin to lose sight of who they are beyond their body.

The truth is that our culture is lying to you. It's packaging sexuality and impurity in beautiful wrapping paper and a shimmery bow. It's telling you that these are the things that everyone is doing, and everyone who is doing them is having a far better time than you. But it's not true. The young woman who is admired only for her body feels lonely and disconnected from real relationship. The teenage girl who has given herself away behind the bleachers discovers is now the talk of the football team and is mortified by what too many guys seem to know about her. She's heartbroken over what feels like betrayal. And the lonely girl who turned to pornography thinking it was a harmless thing is now battling loneliness, addiction, and shame to the depths of her being.

Things are not as they seem, and that's exactly what our God talks about in Scripture as well. He warns us, "There is a way that appears to be right, but in the end it leads to death" (Proverbs 14:12).

So when you see a girl casually sleep with her boyfriend on TV, or you hear the songs that talk of only the delights of casual sex or wild hook ups, remember the truth. Remember your God. Remember his protection and the reality of where these things can lead you. Culture is selling you a broken product. Don't buy it. TV characters may seem to breeze through life with joy and connection—but those same TV characters are paid good money to keep you envying their world. Their manufactured, safe, fake world. Fight the lies of culture with truth, and don't buy what they're selling.

> **"I'd be inspired by something that would remind me that it's okay to be different and not fit in."**
> *~Emilie*

WHAT OUR HEARTS LONG FOR

Choosing purity in the physical realm gets tough when some good-looking guy tells you how beautiful you are—especially if you hunger for that type of reaction. If you feel insecure (and most of us do about something), it feels good to hear that your eyes melt him to his core or your smile makes him weak at the knees. Maybe you've crossed lines simply to hear kind words, letting those compliments unlock what you've held close.

I know this sounds dumb, but I remember being totally shocked that a guy might say things just to get me to do things with him. I looked at my friend Susan, "What? Really? He would lie to me?"

Duh.

I was embarrassed that I fell for it, that I let my values be swayed because someone thought my eyes looked like limpid pools. What are limpid pools anyway? I had no clue, but I felt beautiful and I bought every word.

So you have the culture pressuring you to pursue things outside of purity, but then if your longing to be found beautiful is especially deep, it can tip the scales into even poorer decisions.

But God had a solution. All along he had a way out from that longing to validate your beauty in someone else's eyes. God himself finds you beautiful. God delights in who you are. If you stay close to him, if you're taking time to spend with him, he is more than able to give you a sense of peace about who you are and how beautiful you are to him.

If only it were that easy, right? If only you could tilt your head toward heaven and see God's smile through the clouds or hear his whisper saying, "I love you, you're beautiful! Love those gorgeous eyes and that bright smile!" If that were the case, "finding your value in Christ," would be as easy as glancing skyward. Unfortunately, it doesn't work like that. And for many of us, it doesn't really matter if God finds us beautiful. We think something along these lines: *That's just like saying that my mom thinks I'm pretty. Well, of course she does. Moms are supposed to think their children are beautiful. God is no different—he has to think I'm beautiful. He made me! I want to find someone else to tell me I'm beautiful, because then I'll know it's really true.*

Does that sound anything like you? It was a lot like I was … I wanted to "find my value in Jesus" but I didn't know how to do it, and since it felt good to be found attractive by guys, I went that route—even if it meant small compromises. But it doesn't have to be that way. There is a way to live as a someone loved and valued by God, and for that to be more than enough for your hungry heart. It looks like this: Talk to him. Talk to God and tell him where you've been trying to find the heart of your value (because, yes, it will make a difference):

God, I know I've been finding my value in words. I know that I depend on compliments to feel good about myself. Too much of my world is tied to whether I am really seen by the guys in my life. I need you. I'm too dependent. I need you to fill me with your love. Will you please fill that place in me? Teach me to fall in love with you, to live in your love, to pursue you and remind myself of your truth so that I don't ever compromise my pure identity just to get a quick fix of flattering talk.

Be real. Talk to your Savior. And then apply his truth:

> You were designed on purpose. God knew what he was doing when he made you. (Paraphrase of Psalm 139:13.)

> You are a work of art. God looks at you and thinks, "I did a good job on that one!" (Paraphrase of Psalm 139:14.)

> You are the apple of his eye. He thinks the world
> of you. (Paraphrase of Psalm 17:8.)

When you apply truth from the Bible, also remind your-self of our first battle: the culture and popular media. It's tempting to look to the media to find out the definition of beauty—but you have to remember that God looks at some-thing completely different. He looks at the heart (see 1 Samuel 16:7). When we are in our right mind, so do we. We all know someone who is the picture of physical perfection but whose heart is as cold as ice. We can almost picture their future when their physical beauty fades and there is nothing left behind those cold eyes. On the flip side, think of an older woman you truly love and admire in this world—maybe she's your grandmother, aunt, or an older woman in the church. Think of what you love about that person. You may picture a warm face with gracious eyes and a tender smile. You might also picture the wrinkles, age spots, and maybe even the round belly. Do the wrinkles detract from beauty? No. Her beauty oozes from every pore because of what lies on the inside.

That is true beauty. A gentle heart, a kind spirit. Those are the things that make a woman beautiful. And those are the kinds of things that come as you know and love a God who knows and loves you back.

Another way God helps us out in this area is through one another. God can use girlfriends in your life to remind you of your beauty even as you remind them of theirs. Be generous with your compliments. Share appreciation. And not just for makeup or clothing, eyes or hair. Take time to notice the hearts of your friends. Affirm them in their good decisions, recognize kindness and hard work. Shake up the world's definition of beauty by allowing God to use you to compliment real beauty in the lives of those around you.

Win the battle against the voices that whisper you are somehow not enough. You are beautiful. Fight the good fight—not just for yourself, but with your friends. Don't ever let a longing to be found beautiful lead you down an impure path. Surround yourself with good friends, go to your God and apply truth. This is a daily battle you can soon leave far behind you as you conquer it with truth.

WHAT OUR BODIES DESIRE

"My biggest struggle is when a boy I really like gets me caught up in the moment. But then I remember all the great things I am so fortunate to have—I don't want to risk any of that for a few stupid minutes."

~Anonymous

Touch, desire, sex ... how could something that feels so good have the potential for so much harm? If only God made our bodies a little more unresponsive. In fact, if I could have sat with God before the beginning of time, I would have asked him to make sex like spinach. *God, forgive me, but couldn't you make it something that's good for you, but not quite so appealing?* But no, the feelings tied to touch and intimacy are intense, and the longings run deep.

It's difficult, isn't it?

But there's a reason God made sex so appealing. There's a reason he made the human body something that would build curiosity and desire in our hearts. God knew exactly what he was doing—he was granting us one of the best gifts imaginable. Sex and touch safely explored in marriage is a true gift. Oh, the fun of being totally naked with someone you're crazy about, knowing you are loved just as you are! To explore one another's bodies without any need for embarrassment—how amazing is that? There's physical pleasure, emotional bonding, and powerful spiritual implications to that union of body and soul. And then to add even more mind-numbing beauty to the whole thing, life is created!

Okay, so if it's so amazing in marriage, couldn't God have made us so we didn't long for sex and touch *before* marriage? If only he had built an internal switch that would turn on sexuality once the wedding bells rang—now *that* would be perfect! But God had a reason for the longings as well. Part of the beauty of sex is longing for it and being willing to hold off for that special person. Part of the beauty is turning away from online temptation or physical exploration with someone else in order to wait for your man.

Think of it this way: Imagine your boyfriend is overseas, fighting in a war. He's waging battle, putting his life at risk, and now it's time to come home. Suddenly he is taken captive and is being held in a prisoner of war camp. Now imagine that your man is the heroic and valiant type. He breaks through enemy lines, dodges bullets and landmines, tosses aside a couple of enemies through hand-to-hand combat, and manages to keep himself hidden in the brush for the final miles. And the whole time, he's been thinking of you. He wants to get home to you and he's willing to do whatever it takes to get there.

Now imagine another guy who lives down the road. He wants to come see you, but hey, he's busy. Would you mind coming over to see him?

Compare the two. The man who fought every battle to come home to you is definitely going to hold a special place in your heart. You're going to meet him at the airport in your prettiest outfit, thrilled to have him home and in your arms.

The guy who couldn't get off his couch to see you? You'll probably let him stay there, alone, thank you very much.

As you fight for your own purity, as you push through the feelings that wage war against you every day, you are doing so with an end in sight. You are willing to wage the battle because you want to honor our God and you want to experience an amazing connection with the man of your dreams. You are giving God the gift of obedience and your future husband the gift of fighting the good fight. You do not have to give in to every emotion that dances across your heart—and no matter how you've lived before, *from this point forward* you can be that valiant woman who chooses to sacrifice today for what will be beautiful, rich, and enticing tomorrow. And what a gift you will be able to give your man as you tell him of the battles you fought to guard your mind, keep your hands to yourself, and wait for his touch ...

How much that will mean to him! And how much that will mean to your God—that you chose to trust and believe his ways, that you battled your physical longings and did what was best despite the deep desire that swept over you. God will be beaming with pride as you go into your future marriage with deep passion for your man and a pure heart ready to love, live, and serve in pure devotion to your God for the rest of your days.

Flee the evil desires of youth and pursue righteousness, faith, love and peace, along with those who call on the Lord out of a pure heart.

2 Timothy 2:22

BUT I'M IN LOVE!

Janelle couldn't get him out of her head. He was the first thing that popped into her mind when she woke up and the last thing she thought of when she went to bed. She spent half the day doodling his name and the other half dreaming of being in his arms. Every portion of her day was wrapped around her first love, Devon. They'd both committed to purity in their early teens, but the lines were getting blurry the longer they dated. "I'm just so in love with him," Janelle wrote in her journal. "I want to be close to him. I don't know how the timing could be any more perfect."

Physical longings are one thing, but love takes things to a whole different level. Being in love won't cause you to sway in your online boundaries, but it can sure cause you to cave in on your physical boundaries. This is the time when you start thinking things like:

Well, we're going to get married one day anyway.

I've never felt like this before.

We've been together so long and I love him so much—I want him to be my first.

When love comes knocking, all the strong rationale for making pure choices can go right out the window. But let me take you back to our first few chapters and the greater love that is leading you to take a different course. The only way to battle the feeling of being in love is to draw on that greater love. Remember the reasons God calls you both to purity: for your protection, blessing, and future, because he loves you and wants the very best for both of you.

So when the pressure of being in love sweeps in to take you away from your values, fight it with truth. And be careful not to fall into the trap that it's you and your man against the world. When you place your love for your boyfriend above your love for family, God, and all others, you put yourself into a very vulnerable place. You'll be all the more likely to let those feelings take you to places you never intended to go. Just remember, you don't have to go everywhere your feelings want to take you.

Finally, when it comes to feelings—physical or emotional—remind yourself of this truth often: your God has a best life in mind for you. Doing what feels good won't be the key to unlocking that best; following God is the key. Ask him to give you a heart to really understand this reality and then ask him for the strength to live it out.

Feelings have nothing on you. Fight them. Remember Jeremiah 17:9: "The heart is deceitful above all things." Don't give in. Ask for God's strength to help when you feel swept away in the battle.

Feelings go away. The sense of accomplishment when you override them for a greater goal—doesn't.

BUT OTHER CHRISTIANS ARE DOING IT

"I'd be inspired if I had more friends who believed in purity. It's tough to be surrounded by friends who are

great people, but they're having sex with their boyfriends when they know they shouldn't."

~Jennifer

"My parents are divorced," said Mattie, "and both of them are living with other people. It's hard for me to listen to them when they tell me that I should wait until marriage. Here they are, both having sex outside of marriage ... Why shouldn't I?"

"My friend says she's a Christian, but she's going to move in with her boyfriend before the wedding. What am I supposed to do with that?"

"My friend walked in the room and her brother was checking out pornography on the computer. They're both in youth group together and it really freaked her out."

As the world gets more and more accepting of certain types of behavior—pornography, sex outside of marriage, online relationships—it makes it very hard to take a stand against the tide. Some days it can feel like anyone and everyone has let you down, like no one stands for what is good and right ... and that in itself can build a temptation to join the crowd.

"I was just tired of being the good girl," Jane said. "Everyone around me was giving in, so why shouldn't I?"

It matters! It matters more than you know. Especially when others who say they love Jesus are falling by the wayside, it matters all the more that *you* stand firm. Even though I was making my own bad decisions, I distinctly remember looking at believers around me and feeling disappointed by their choices. "No one really lives it out, God. No one lives it every day." Rather than hearing a resounding, "You're right, so you're right to go your own way too, Elsa," I felt like he whispered, "Then why don't you? Why don't you live out the reality of my love, Elsa?"

You can look all day at other lives and see how they are giving up and walking away, but is that what God is asking of you? Or is he calling you to live your life in such a way that others look at you and say, "Jesus is real. I can tell by what he's done in her life …"

Show them what real faith looks like. Show them purity. Live it yourself, no matter what has been lived around you.

> **"It seems like all my friends have sex with their boyfriends. They talk about it like it's okay, and it doesn't bother them. Sometimes I think to myself that if that's how they feel, I probably wouldn't care either. But then I go to God and he reminds me that it's not okay and that it's not for the best, and he has something better for me. He reminds me of the truth."**
>
> *~Anonymous*

BOLDLY OWN YOUR JOURNEY

Yes, there are pressures in this world, pressures coming in from every side. Culture is one voice, hunger to be found beautiful cries out with another, and what people model around us can come in as a high-pitched squeal. But this is about you. This is your journey and there is only one voice you need to pay attention to:

My sheep listen to my voice; I know them, and they follow me.

John 10:27

Listen for your God, the one who knows you and loves you best. Don't let any excuse keep you from his path. Remember that he not only loves you with a fierce, powerful, and protective love, he equips you to face every battle that may come your way: "The righteous cry out, and the LORD hears them; he delivers them from all their troubles" (Psalm 34:17).

This is your opportunity to live a life different from the rest. This is your chance to stand and choose your own path. Yes, there are pressures pushing you toward brokenness, but there is blessing and strength as you move forward along the path you know to be right. James 4:7 reminds you to resist the Devil and he will flee from you. In our God, you are strong. Fight the bad guys off! Even if you've been weak in the past, that doesn't mean you have to be weak in the future. Cry out, call out, lean on a strength that's bigger than you, and then move forward in joy and confidence. Boldly own your journey. It doesn't matter what a single other person chooses to do, you are choosing to follow your God.

And he is beaming with pride.

DISCUSSION/JOURNAL QUESTIONS

Which pressure do you experience the most? Cultural? Physical longing? Desire to be found beautiful? That I-give-up feeling because of how others are living? Explain why you think this pressure has been such a big part of your life.

What is one specific thing you can do to get rid of that pressure? Filter out some of the media in your life? Talk to God about your value? Be specific and share what steps you will take.

When you imagine boldly owning your own journey, how does it make you feel? What inspires you or scares you about walking a different road from those around you?

What do you think God would say to you if you chose to fight the good fight of faith? Be specific.

CHAPTER EIGHT

THE EMOTIONAL TRIP

When feelings take you for a ride

In the last chapter we talked about love and physical desire, but choosing purity is more than stuffing those feelings down, acknowledging a greater love, and fighting the good fight of faith. God wired you as an emotional being. You're amazing that way. You are capable of deep passion, profound joy, delightful abandon, and righteous anger. As a woman, you have a unique capacity to feel deeply and with God's help, those emotions will drive you to do wonderful things: love your God, connect with your man, care for your children one day, and right the wrongs that take place in the world. There is such powerful beauty in your God-given wiring, and in the right environment, you can transform the world with what lies inside of you.

Unfortunately, there is a flip side. I'm going to share with you four different scenarios—see if you can figure out how emotion (beyond lust or love), played into the choices of these young women.

Joni slammed the door and walked outside. She was so sick of fighting over every little thing and so tired of being told what to do. It's like her parents couldn't seem to grasp that she was growing up. *I'm almost eighteen*, she screamed in her brain. *Don't you get it? I need to make my own choices!*

Joni heard a familiar tone and glanced down at her phone. It was Roger. She picked up.

"Yeah?" Her tone was harsh.

"Whoa, what's the matter with you?"

"Nothing. Sorry. I just wanted to do something, and my parents are acting like I'm still ten years old. It drives me crazy."

"Well, I just wanted to see if you wanted to go to DJ's with me tonight. He's having a couple of people over."

Joni knew this was about more than hanging out with a few friends. Roger had liked her for a long time and she'd been putting him off. He wasn't really her type. He liked to drink and he was known for being a player. Her parents didn't like him either; they'd made that very clear. Joni wasn't supposed to spend time with him. And until now, she hadn't really wanted to …

She hesitated. "Well?" he pushed.

Joni looked over her shoulder at the house and could see her mom through the window, staring out at her with her arms folded.

Joni felt the irritation immediately rise up. "Yeah, I can go."

"Your parents won't care?"

"My parents won't know. I'll meet you at DJ's at nine." Joni hung up the phone and felt a flush of triumph.

You can't control me …

The very next morning, Joni sat in her bedroom, flushed with regret. Why had she gone to DJ's? Why had she let

Roger touch her like that? Yeah, she had pushed him away, and yes, she'd come home and climbed back through her window in the middle of the night.

But how did the whole thing even happen in the first place?

Tara bit her lip to keep from crying. Her best friend, Kayla, had moved to another state a few weeks ago and had already seemed to forget their friendship. Tara was in a new school and hadn't met a single soul who seemed to care. Her parents were busy all the time and her brother seemed to have plugged in with a zillion different friends before school even started.

The loneliness felt tangible, like a weight on her shoulders and a physical ache in her heart.

Tara flipped on the family computer and checked her messages. Her parents were upstairs and her brother was out, so she checked out another site she'd overheard a couple of other kids talking about. It was an online community where you could create an avatar that looked however you wanted her to look. *I'll just check it out*, Tara thought. She could tell from the entrance to the site that most people weren't exactly modest in dressing the online version of themselves. Tara felt a little twinge of concern but quickly brushed it to the side. *None of it is real anyway.*

Within just a few weeks, Tara's mind was wrapped up in her new world. Curiosity had led her to some dark places in that online community and she was surprised and intrigued by how the interaction seemed so real. She knew her parents wouldn't approve, so she snuck to the computer in the middle of the night or when she was certain everyone was busy in other rooms of the house. When her parents caught her, she was surprised at how easily the lies flowed. Seriously, this was the first time she'd been here. No, she didn't like it. Yes, she understood the dangers of talking to people she didn't know. Sorry, it won't happen again.

So weird. Her parents had loved her for her whole life and she was protecting a group of people she didn't even know. Sure, every once in a while she would worry who was on the other end of her avatar friends, but most of the time she let herself get lost.

It wasn't until months into her new addiction, as more and more lies flowed from her lips, that Tara realized she was no longer making the choices of the nice Christian girl she'd always considered herself to be. Everything she was doing was orchestrated around her new world—no matter the cost.

How did I let things come to this?

Raven missed her true love, Alex. She and Alex had been together since the seventh grade and had broken up just before her senior year in high school. They'd done everything together. They knew each other's families, friends, hopes, and dreams. They'd talked on the phone until the wee hours of the morning and held hands for the first time at an old-fashioned drive-in theater.

And then out of the blue Alex broke up with her. To Raven, it seemed like everything was going fine. Yeah, they fought a little more than usual, and true, he seemed to talk about that Leslie girl in his physics class, but Raven never thought it would come to this.

Now she walked down the hall and saw the two of them together and it about killed her. How could he find someone else so quickly? How could he walk away like they didn't have anything together?

And the worst part? Raven had just done something really stupid with her best friend, Tyler. They'd been friends for a long time and she didn't know—until *that* night—that Tyler liked her as more than just a friend. He'd leaned in to kiss Raven just as she was talking about Alex. And instead of pushing him away like she absolutely should have, Raven had melted into him. Oh, to feel a warm and affectionate touch. She closed her eyes and imagined it was Alex, back again in her life, touching her cheek and telling her how much he loved her.

Raven wanted to say that she had no idea how the rest of it happened, but she would be lying. She'd let things go way too far with Tyler just because she missed Alex.

Now she had no idea what to do.

How could I have let this happen?

Ruth felt bad for him. Nick had always been a few rungs behind everyone else on the social ladder. He was a nice enough guy, but he always seemed a little awkward, a little uncomfortable around people his own age. Nick had started texting Ruth after a youth group lock-in. He'd shared with the group that he didn't have many friends and Ruth's heart went out to him. She hated the thought that he was so lonely and she wanted to make it better for him.

The first time he texted her a provocative message, she thought it was a mistake. "Nick," she texted back, "what are you doing?"

She didn't hear from him for a few days, but then he texted again, this time just a normal message. Ruth breathed a sigh of relief. "You okay?"

"Yeah," he said.

He went on to text how he had never kissed a girl and didn't think he ever would. He asked if he could text her just a few random things, "just to see what it's like to have someone in my life."

Ruth felt a wave of compassion. What would be the harm if they just texted a few things back and forth? It seemed like the right thing to do, he was so lonely—he just needed someone to pretend with. How could that be wrong?

It began with just a few texts here and there. They made Ruth uncomfortable, but they also stirred up feelings that she liked. She found herself responding, even as she told herself she shouldn't. Their messages grew more and more graphic and she was surprised at how quickly she fell into the sexual banter.

One day her mom picked up her phone and Ruth jumped to grab it from her hand. She was surprised by the racing fear and deep shame she felt come over her as she tried to keep her mom from reading the messages.

This is not who I am, she thought to herself.

How did I end up here?

LIFE: THE EMOTIONAL RIDE

Can you see it? Can you see how these well-meaning girls landed in situations they never anticipated? They didn't start down their paths with the thought that they would make the choices they did, but that's where they ended up.

So what emotions made them vulnerable to assaults on their purity? For Joni, it was anger. For Tara, loneliness. For Raven, it was rejection, and for Ruth it was the initial pull of compassion. Most of us wouldn't connect anger, loneliness, rejection, or compassion to impurity. Talk to most people and they'd boil it down into one emotion: lust. You can almost picture the woman with the spectacles and the cane, wagging her finger in your face. "When you lust, then you enter into evil!" But that's not true. Lust is typically a symptom of something deeper going on. It's a good idea to look at what might be beneath it.

Are you lonely? Angry? Feeling rejected? Feeling sorry for someone?

There are other emotions that can take you down an impure path: sadness, a sense of abandonment, hunger for connection ... The list goes on and on.

So what can you do to make sure you don't feel an emotion and then head down a bad path as a result? Let's look at some tools you can put in your emotional toolbox, habits that will equip you to control your emotions and funnel them toward good, rather than toward choices you might regret.

BE AWARE AND ASK FOR GOD'S HELP

Get in the habit of asking yourself, What am I feeling right now? Am I happy? Sad? Lonely? Angry? See if you can pinpoint why you might be feeling that way.

Think about Joni's story. She might have stopped in that moment and thought, *Okay, I'm angry at my parents. I feel like they don't let me do anything and it bugs me to no end.* Rather than stuffing that emotion and then letting it lead to a bad choice, Joni could have chosen a different path. First, Joni could acknowledge her anger. Then she could whisper a prayer to her God, like, *Lord, you know I'm angry. I'm not feeling or thinking good things right now. Please help me to handle this in the right way.*

If Joni's parents were reasonable people (and most parents are), Joni could have then gone to them and shared her heart. "Mom, Dad, I feel like you don't trust me. I'm almost eighteen and I would love to be more independent, but I don't want to make you angry in the process. Can we talk about it?"

Most parents will respond well when their child wants to talk. Now if Joni's parents weren't emotionally healthy, she could still begin in the same place, acknowledge she is angry and ask for God's help, and then go to her journal or to a friend and process her emotions.

Being aware of your feelings and asking for God's help in handling them are huge first steps in making pure decisions in the midst of chaotic emotions.

Think about Tara. She was lonely and ended up looking for online relief. She could have made some better choices as well. The day she was sitting at the computer and felt that uncomfortable feeling, she had an opportunity to ask herself, *Why am I choosing this? I know this isn't right, so God, what's inside of me that's making me want to push forward?*

God may have led Tara's thoughts to the reality that she was missing her best friend and not yet connected to anyone at school. Tara then could have thought it through to the truth: *Do online relationships really help me feel connected? Or can I choose something different?* From there, maybe Tara could go to her parents or her brother, tell them she was lonely, and ask for some help in getting plugged in.

So first, be aware. Ask yourself what you're feeling and see if you can figure out why. Second, ask God to help you handle the emotion in a healthy way. Scripture never says you won't get angry, it just says not to sin in that anger (see Ephesians 4:26). Scripture also acknowledges loneliness, and reminds you that you have a God who will never leave you or forsake you (see Deuteronomy 31:8). Learning to call out to him in those lonely moments will save you a lot of heartache.

Now keep in mind that most people, even adults, are still learning this process. I don't expect you to walk away from this book and get it all perfect. Can you imagine? You set the book down, get in a heated argument with your brother, get super angry, and then *voila!* All because of this book, you pause in the midst of that intense emotion with an ever-so-wise look on your face—and after a slight pause, you glance up, fold your hands, and pray to God instead of clobbering the brother you were about to clobber.

Unfortunately, it's just not that easy. Emotion, by its very nature, is intense. It's very, very difficult to stop mid-anger/mid-loneliness/mid-rejection to analyze the emotion, pray, and come to some sort of holy response.

It's okay. Remember that it's a process and start by doing a daily check-in. Look back at your day and see if you can figure out what you were feeling and how you responded to those feelings. Ask God to give you eyes to see where your emotions might be getting you into trouble. As you do that on a daily basis, you'll become more aware, and as you become more aware, you'll be better able to stop and ask God for help in responding to whatever might sideline you. As you are faithful to the process, you'll find yourself making a whole lot fewer decisions out of stark emotion and a whole lot more decisions out of wisdom and connection with the one who loves you most.

BE INTENTIONAL WITH YOUR RESPONSE

Let's take a look at our second two scenarios. Raven was feeling rejected and missing her boyfriend, so she let herself get physically involved with her best friend, Tyler. Ruth had some healthy compassion for Nick's loneliness, but she expressed that compassion in a very unhealthy way by texting him inappropriate messages. The first thing both Raven and Ruth could have done was to acknowledge what they were feeling and then ask God for help in dealing with it. Once they did that, they could look for a healthy solution: For Raven, more than a set of strong arms, she needed to let herself have a good cry. She was missing her first love, but because he "moved on" so quickly, she figured she would just run to the next set of available arms as well. Instead, she should have patted herself on the back for loving so deeply, taken some time to journal or talk to her friends, and let herself feel the sadness. Grieving is not a horrible thing, feeling sad is not the worst thing that can happen. Making a poor choice to avoid the feeling is much worse.

Ruth had the same option. She felt compassion for her friend, Nick. She could take that compassion to God and ask him, "Lord, what should I do to help Nick? Show me how to help him." In doing that, when Nick sent her something inappropriate, God would have helped Ruth to stand firm. She'd sense the strong uneasiness that God can bring when we're about to do something dumb. She could have then said, "Nick, I know you're lonely, but doing this kind of stuff isn't going to help either one of us. Why don't you start showing up to youth group and I'll introduce you around to some of the guys. They're pretty cool to hang out with."

Again, like recognizing emotion and running to God, choosing a healthy response will be a process. It won't go perfectly and you might make some mistakes along the way. But the reality remains that if you are intentional in dealing with your emotions, then you will live pure. You'll be letting God use emotions to draw you to himself and you'll be letting emotions do the work they were meant to do. See, emotions aren't evil, they simply let us know that something needs to be dealt with. For example, God lets us feel lonely to prompt us toward healthy relationship with people. He lets us feel anger so we'll point that passion toward righting wrongs. And when we experience rejection or compassion, in his hands those emotions can spur us on to reach out to the rejected and the hurting with his love.

PURE LOVE

"I believe God asks us to live pure lives so that we can realize life is all about him. Yes, he gave us things that will give us physical pleasure, but they are gifts. God has given us value, so living pure lives can give us perspective on how all creation centers around him."

~Sarah

I have good news. Intense emotion can take you down an impure path, but intense emotion can also make you strong and unshakable in your convictions. When you express intense emotion to your God, who formed you and loves you,

you'll draw closer to him. And if you're close to him, it'll be a lot tougher for anything to pull you away. Think about it. God is crazy about you, and we spent a whole lot of time in the first chapters talking about what it looks like to feel God's love—how important it is to be real with him, to look for his hand in the world around you, to notice those God kisses that might come in the form of a sunset, the hug of a friend, a song on the radio. Loving him back will only make your relationship all the more real and your pure heart all the more strong.

Let me share a little love story with you to help drive this home.

I knew the night Brian was going to propose to me. I knew it the moment that he invited me on the big, fancy date. He told me to get dressed up. He told me we were going to an expensive restaurant, and he sounded nervous. I'd never heard Brian nervous before.

It took me forever to get ready. I was a single mom, so my daughter, Sam, and I shut ourselves in my closet as we tried to find something for me to wear. Sam held up different outfits to my chin. "Too sparkly," she'd proclaim and toss it aside. "Too frumpy," she'd declare, and off that one would go. Finally, she responded, "Ah, just perfect." We settled on the black dress that was classy and, miracle of miracles, trimmed me down by a pound or two.

Loved it.

Brian came to pick me up and he looked incredible in his jacket and tie. He drove me to the restaurant, the kind where they don't trust you to put the cloth napkins on your lap by yourself. It's true. You have to raise your hands and they put the napkin on your lap for you.

How swanky. How lovely.

Before we even had a chance to look at the menu, and long before Brian proposed, the waitress came out with a bottle of champagne. I guess Brian had told them his big plan for the evening, so she walked up to the table and smiled big at me. "Congratulations …!"

I could sense Brian making all kinds of hand motions to the left of me. The woman stopped and realized he hadn't asked me the big question yet. She looked at me. She looked at Brian. She looked back at me and tried to save the moment. "Congratulations … uh … on your night out!"

Wow! I looked at Brian and played dumb. "They really celebrate people coming to their restaurant, huh?"

Brian nodded, little beads of sweat on his forehead.

After dinner and before dessert, Brian grabbed hold of my hand and took me outside. We walked over a small bridge on a nearby lake. Right on the center of the bridge he turned, knelt on one knee, told me what he loved about me, and asked me to marry him.

I squealed. I pulled him up to his feet and smooched him right there. "Yes! Yes! Yes!"

He placed the ring on my finger and we turned to look out over the lake. There, right by the bridge, were two swans with their necks arched in the shape of a heart. "No way!" I looked at Brian in delight. "Did you hire them?"

It was a perfect night, a romantic evening to surpass my dreams. Even as I type it now, a smile lingers on my face.

Now imagine if on that special night when Brian got down on one knee and professed his love, imagine if I gave him a distracted smile, turned, and went back into the restaurant. He would have poured out his heart to receive absolutely nothing in response. Our big romantic evening would have stalled out right then and there. No shared laughter, no sweet kiss, no forever love story.

But how often does that happen in our relationship with God? We sense his love in some way, maybe when he helps us with a test, or loves us through a friend's hug, or makes us smile with our favorite song—we'll sense that the God of the universe just intersected our world with a smile—and we'll turn away, missing a moment to respond.

Like Brian professing his love on his knees, God professed his love on the cross, and continues to profess his love in the God kisses that litter our world. Don't let those moments pass. Don't miss that chance to express your love in return! Whisper "I love you." Thank him for the love. Open your heart to his and let that feeling sweep you off your feet.

Every moment like that will build your pure heart. Every give-and-take of real relationship with your loving God will strengthen you on your pure path. Respond. Respond intensely. Let your God-given wiring build your love relationship with Jesus and don't let anything get in the way.

I can remember watching a group of teens worship God one Friday evening. Their love was written on their faces, their passion spilling from every pore. They were so beautiful! I could just imagine God with a big smile on his face, loving them too.

It's a two-way street. As you feel God's love, love him back and watch how your relationship grows. Out of that growth will come your pure heart. Pure love builds a pure life. No way around it.

Blessed are the pure in heart, for they will see God.

Matthew 5:8

DISCUSSION/JOURNAL QUESTIONS

Can you see how emotions like anger, loneliness, rejection, or compassion could impact your choices toward purity? Have you seen this play out (in big or small ways) in your own life?

What step can you take to get a greater grasp on how you respond to emotions? Be specific.

Have you ever thought about loving God back when you sense his love? Explain how this could deepen your relationship with him.

Take a few minutes and share with your group, or write in your journal, how you feel about God right this moment. Share what you love about him today.

CHAPTER NINE

TECHNO SAVVY

Navigating the virtual

Okay, that's it! Throw away your phone, toss your computer, and move to the island of Bora Bora … But wait—only if the tribal people are fully clothed.

That's almost what it feels like, doesn't it? We've talked a couple of times about the dangers of pornography, sexting, and the temptation for anonymous online interaction, so it seems like maybe technology is actually the big EVIL we all need to discard from our lives. Maybe we should just turn in our technologically advanced products and move to that far-off island where we can interact face-to-face and eyeball-to-eyeball.

Tempting, but not very realistic.

Here's the truth: technology in itself is not evil. And God is not surprised by all the advances in our world today. He's not sitting up in heaven wringing his hands and wondering how things got so out of control: *Gosh, I didn't expect they'd learn much beyond how to make a wheel. Now what am I going to do?* God is very aware of what's happening and even better, he actually created the minds that came up with the tools you use.

So looking at the brilliance of our God and the beauty of

his character, it seems to me that he knew exactly what he was doing when he picked the time you would be born into, the technology you'd have, and the tools at your disposal. Even better, he has a plan for how you can use that technology for your good and his glory.

THE GOOD STUFF

Dealing with technology is not about hiding under a rock and plotting how to avoid every assault on your purity. Yes, it's wise to be aware of the dangers of the virtual world (and we'll dive into those a little later in this chapter), but what about all the good things available online? Like researching your future or checking out random YouTube videos that make you laugh or connecting with good friends via social networking? And what if you chose to use some resources online to help build your faith? Find godly encouragement? Or join in the fight for good? Who is to say you couldn't be the next Internet sensation—but on the topic of purity? You could be someone who spurs others on to pure love for their God and pure living in their day-to-day. Remember, purity isn't all about the no, it's figuring out what you can pour your life into that's good, loving, and real. There are lots of books on purity, but where are the places where teens are encouraging teens? Where are the videos that speak truth, and where are teens standing together to bring rampant change for good? This is your time, these advances are your advances! Whether it's a purity pledge that you put together for your friends or a blog on how you can stand for purity after having made some poor choices, it's your story, heart, and passion that can make a difference in the lives of others.

"Are there many other teens out there trying to stand for purity?" one girl asked me when she heard about this book. She wasn't sure there was anyone else actually choosing to fight the good fight.

So maybe it's time to band together and communicate your heart and your story to others. Let's begin by taking a look at where you can find encouragement from young women who are living pure lives out of pure love, as well as some of the amazing things others have done.

First things first: honor your parents. If you're living at home, the boundaries your parents have set for online interaction are the boundaries you need to follow. If you read suggestions in these pages that sound wonderful, but go against a rule your parents have set in place, please honor what they've told you. They know you best and they want to protect you. Even if their restrictions seem unreasonable to you, thank God that they care about your world, and honor what they require of you.

HOW TO FIND ENCOURAGEMENT

You are not alone on this journey. Whether you are pursuing a pure life for the first time, turning away from a broken past to make things right, or determining to live a pure road despite what someone has done to you, you are not alone. Whatever your first steps, there is someone else who has walked in your shoes.

Connect with other teens, and begin by doing research. Plug *Christian teens* or *purity* into a search engine and see what resources come up—online communities, forums, or articles designed to support teens as they commit to pure living.

Wherever you land, always consider the author of the source and see how many teens have found it helpful. If you're concerned about doing that kind of research online, ask a parent or a trusted friend to help you out. Together, you can check out the details on the site: Is it biblical? Is it inspiring? Interactive? Determine if it's a good fit for you and if it is, bookmark it and turn to it when you need an extra boost of encouragement. A safe bet (in addition to other sites you find) is *www.purelovepurelife.com*; you can stop in there for content or to sign up to receive purity blogs in your email.

Another avenue is YouTube, GodTube, or other video venues. Some amazing believers have created powerful videos describing God's love, illustrating Scripture or even encouraging others with straight, authentic God talk. Go there. Check it out. Plug in *God's love* and see what results. Let the creativity of other believers remind you of the loving God who wants real relationship with you. Let the words and images encourage your faith and then take some time responding to God.

Now keep in mind, whether it's a forum or a video, you have to look with discerning eyes. If you run across a video or forum discussion that depicts God as a marshmallow in the sky or a loving spirit that lives inside of a turtle, click the video off. Pay close attention to the content to see if it veers from the Bible, and if it does, find another forum. If you're unsure about a posting, don't be afraid to talk with your parents (if they are believers) or a youth pastor. Ask for help in understanding what's being said. This is a healthy thing to do. As you question things you see or read, you'll grow your faith as you research the truth. Don't be afraid to talk to trusted spiritual advisors *any time* you have a question about faith. It's not bad to question, it's only bad if questions go underground, don't find answers, and leave you with a shaky faith as you move forward into your future.

There's more. If you have this option available, you can download an app with the Bible on it. You can plug in *pure* and strengthen yourself with Scriptures at the drop of a hat. You can download a Bible study and commit to reading it. Invite a friend to read it as well and discuss it over lunch or on a coffee date.

More encouragement can be found in music. My daughter absolutely loves to listen to music. She finds strength in heart-pounding visionary tunes and inspiration in worship music from the heart. Access and listen to music that's going to inspire you, strengthen you, and give you joy when you blare it in your room. By the same token, watch that you don't download tunes that talk about steaming up the back window or dancing super close in a club. I can hear some of you already: "I just love the beat! I don't actually listen to the words ..." But you *do* listen to the words. Your mind actually catches every one and they really do influence how you think and feel about purity. Be wise in this. Be intentional. You have lots of good options. It's not like the olden days where Christian music was about as exciting as granola. Today there are as many Christian artists as there are differences in taste. Find one you like, find *several* you like, and pump that stuff into your brain. It will make a difference.

Remember, you don't have to be passive in your approach to the virtual stuff. You don't simply have to put on a blinder and say, "I'll never look at a computer again!"

Rather, you can use every tool at your fingertips to build your relationship with God, your awareness of his love, and your understanding of his truth.

Encouragement is only a click away.

Find it, let it soak in, and then move on with your day.

You can do this.

CREATING ENCOURAGEMENT FOR OTHERS

"My biggest struggle is telling others about my choice—I'm scared to do that."

~Leslie

Because of the technology available to people from every age and walk of life, the opportunity to make a difference in the lives of others multiplies in powerful ways.

A young man in Atlanta heard about the reality of human slavery still in existence today. At a young age, he determined to do something about it. He created an organization called Loose Change to Loosen Chains and raised, well, loose change to loosen chains. His passion for forgotten modern slaves, and his message presented on a social network page, inspired other teens to join his cause. Thousands upon thousands of dollars came in because of his deep compassion and singular focus to do something about an issue close to his heart.

Two fourteen-year-old girls joined together when they found out about the horrific conditions for AIDS victims in Africa. They created a basketball competition in their small town and called it "Hoops for Hope." They raised a good amount of money and a whole lot of awareness for victims and their families in Zambia. One boy who influenced them: another teen with a website and a platform who encourages people all over the country to use basketballs to change lives.

Another young man was appalled to find out that many African families didn't have access to clean water. At the age of seven, he began raising funds for his first well, and throughout his teenage years he built his passion into a worldwide campaign that continues to raise money and build wells for those without access to clean water.

One young woman did a project on the sanctity of human life for her school. Her mother videotaped her as she shared her passion, and once the video went online, this young girl suddenly had a nationwide platform to share of her heartfelt concern for the unborn.

Don't underestimate what God can do through passion and ingenuity, coupled with the technology of today. Here are a few ideas to spur your creativity, but don't stop with these. Come up with your own plan to funnel all that pure, positive energy into sharing God's heart on this topic.

> *Ways to say no:* Create a YouTube or GodTube video with your friends on ways to get out of uncomfortable situations. Whether it's role-playing a response to an inappropriate text or the "top ten things a girl can say to a persistent boy," be creative and have fun with it, but give some real tools that other girls will find helpful.

> *You're not the only one:* Be bold in your dedication to pure living. Create a video, by yourself or with friends, that shares your heart to love God with all that lies inside of you. Sometimes just

seeing that another teen is living out her faith in a real way can be inspiring for others.

Text encouragement: **Commit to standing with your girlfriends as they seek to live out this life. Text each other a check-in message if one of you goes out on a date. Keep tabs on each other and give lots of enthusiastic encouragement when your friends choose well.**

Create a page, forum, or website: **Recruit others to communicate their passion for pure living. Share ideas on how to connect with God, grow your faith, or stand firm in your commitment to physical purity. Join with other teens in signing a pledge to help each other and hold each other accountable.**

Start a blog: **If you like to write, kick off your own blog. Or if you have a single blog post you might want to share, submit it to us at www.purelove-purelife.com. If it's something we haven't covered, and you cover it in a unique and creative way, you could be a guest blogger for us!**

Here's the reality: you are unlimited in your opportunity to make a huge difference in other lives. Pure living is allowing the pure love of our God to pour out from you into the lives of others. If clean wells or unborn babies or orphans in Africa stir your heart, pour that pure energy into that outlet. Take technology and use it as a tool in God's hands to inform and equip others to join you in your passion.

The bottom line is that with some research, you can find

encouragement and inspiration from others to live out purity. And with ingenuity and wisdom, you can find ways to offer that same encouragement to friends or classmates in your circle and, if God calls, around the world.

SAFETY IN THE VIRTUAL WORLD

I want to remind you of something very important. If you consider moving forward in finding encouragement in the virtual world or offering it to others, please be safe. Don't head off and make a video without your parent's consent. They can help you make sure to protect yourself from any online predators. While technology is a tool, it can also be a danger. Be very wise and make sure you have some trusted adults in your corner to help you navigate any safety issues.

Whenever you interact in virtual ways (computer, phone, iPad, etc.), there are things you need to keep right at the forefront of your mind. Let's go over a few of them to make sure you avoid some common dangers and pitfalls.

NEVER GIVE PERSONAL INFORMATION TO OTHERS

Be guarded. Whether it's through texting, instant chats, or anywhere online, don't give out personal information. Even if someone is talking about purity and appears to be the picture of angelic perfection, be very guarded. The huge danger of the virtual world is its anonymity. Anyone can be whoever he or she wants to be. You may think you're discussing life with a thirteen-year-old girl and only find out later that it's a forty-six-year-old man. Be cautious. Never give out any personal information.

NEVER SEND PHOTOS OF YOURSELF TO ANYONE

This is similar to giving out personal information, but be guarded with your photos. The biggest danger is when you are in a dating relationship and you're invited to send a naked picture of yourself. The whole "I'll show you mine if you show me yours" happens all the time. If you haven't been asked to do this, you likely will be. Don't ever do it. Ever. Once that picture leaves your device, it's out there in cyber-space, and you never know where it will end up. I recently read in the newspaper of a young woman who sent a photo of herself to her boyfriend. He forwarded it along to one friend and before she knew it, her entire class at school had seen it. This young woman's humiliation was so deep, she ended up committing suicide.

Remember, your body is your own, reserved to be seen by one person and one person only—the man God has for you. Guard it until that time. Don't send photos of yourself. Don't expose yourself to that kind of potential pain. And if you've done it already, commit to yourself that you won't do it ever again. It just isn't worth it.

Along these same lines, avoid talking sexually via text as well. We've already touched on this, but when you spend a lot of time talking dirty with people, it's very, very difficult for purity to hold your heart. Your thoughts will be shaped by the images you've read about, and you'll spend a lot of time thinking about what you should say in response and how the words make you feel. And then knowing that it's not the way God would want you to relate (because you're essentially using each other for physical pleasure), you're more likely to hide from him and miss seeing the God kisses in your world. It's tough to feel loved by a good, pure, and holy God when you are talking in cheap ways to another human being.

God has so much better for you. Don't settle for less!

AVOID PORNOGRAPHY AT ALL COSTS

We've discussed this, but it's important to touch on it in this chapter as well. You might hear from people, possibly even Christians, that pornography is harmless. They might say something like, "Well, it's natural. This is the way we all are and there's nothing wrong with looking at other people." But it's not natural. Or good. Or healthy in any way. Don't worry, you will get to satisfy your curiosity about the human body and enjoy all kinds of sexual exploration in the safety of your marriage. And if God doesn't call you to marriage, he'll help you with the desire. Pornography is not a "healthy alternative" to sex. It stirs up lust, and lust reduces a whole person into a body to be checked out and undressed with our eyes … a reality so far from the truth. Pornography breaks God's heart: for the participant, because they are being publicly used and dishonored, and for the viewer, because he or she has turned someone's body into entertainment, forgetting that the body holds the heart of someone who matters to God.

If you struggle in this area already, please ask for help. Please talk to someone you trust. If not your parents, then a youth pastor or a godly adult in your world. It's not unusual to get lost in this stuff without ever intending it to happen—what started as curiosity can sometimes get the best of us. So talk to someone and get help to move beyond it. Fessing up may be tough at first, but it's a whole lot better than continuing to feed an addiction that will suck the life out of your relationship with God and others. Talk to someone. You'll feel a thousand times better if you do.

AVOID ONLINE DATING

I met Brian in Arizona. He lived in Ohio and I lived in Colorado. We met at a conference for singles in Phoenix. In the Bible, Jacob found Rachel while she was watering sheep in the middle of the desert. God is not concerned with geography, circumstance, livestock, or anything else. If he wants to bring two people together, he can make it happen.

So is online dating wrong? If you are a younger teen reading this, I would say yes. Simply because there are so many predators trolling those sites, you could easily end up falling in love with someone who only wants to do you harm. Stay away. It's truly not worth the risk. For older teens, eighteen and over, I wouldn't necessarily say it's sinful, but I would say that you don't need to go there. God has you covered, and as it is for the younger crowd, the risks of online dating far outweigh the potential benefit.

Another potentially dangerous scenario is what online dating does to your heart and your perceptions. Think about it: You're checking out pictures, likes, and dislikes, and evaluating people based on very little information. It can be a quick and shallow journey to judging folks based solely on their appearance. Also, online dating makes it easy to date a couple of people at one time. Since you can "date" as many people as you can find, you're training your heart to spread your love over multiple relationships at the same time. So what's going to happen when you marry and you get a little bored or uneasy or unhappy with the one you're with? Because you've trained yourself to go from one heart to another, it will make it that much easier to abandon your spouse in pursuit of something a little more exciting.

You can relax in the dating process. You don't have to force a thing. God has you, and if you're not dating now, you don't have to look for someone new. Just enjoy time on your own, time with God, and time with friends.

NOW YOU'RE EQUIPPED

You know the dangers, you know the things you need to do to stay safe, so now you can think again about the positive ways you can use technology to inspire your pure journey. Take some time with that thought. Talk to your parents or another trusted adult, talk with your friends and bat some ideas around. Come up with unique ways to use technology in a God-honoring way, to pour out your story, your purity, and your life as an inspiration to others.

DISCUSSION/JOURNAL QUESTIONS

Have you ever thought about ways you could find inspiration and encouragement using technology? What is one thing you can do to help you on your own journey? (Access Scripture verses? Check out videos on God's love? Connect to a Christian teen forum? Subscribe to the blogs from *www.purelovepurelife.com*?)

What are some ways that you might be able to use technology to inspire others? (Text your friends? Create a funny skit and post it? Write a blog?)

What steps can you take to keep yourself safe in our virtual world? Are there any things you're doing now that compromise your safety? What steps can you take to fix that?

CHAPTER TEN

BETTER THAN THE FAIRY TALES

Pure marriage to the one you love

There was my groom. He looked so good in his black tuxedo, white shirt, and blue tie, I couldn't take my eyes off him as I walked down the aisle on my father's arm. I felt beautiful. My wedding gown was fitted in just the right ways, jewels shimmered, and a long bow and beautiful train flowed behind me. Everything was perfect, down to my pedicured toes peeking out from beneath my gown. I went barefoot for both divine and selfish reasons. Just like Moses needed to get rid of his shoes by the burning bush, I was taking off my shoes for this holy moment. And, okay, if I'm brutally honest, uncomfortable shoes had never been my thing and the idea of padding down the church aisle in my bare tootsies made me smile.

It was perfect. Better than I could have dreamed …

And as I stood there, facing the pastor with my future husband holding my hand, I was grinning from ear to ear. I was marrying my best friend in the whole world. We'd made pure choices as individuals, pure choices throughout our dating, and we were headed pure into our marriage.

I couldn't wait to wrap my arms around him with uninhibited passion, to culminate what we'd been waiting for ...

I won't go into details (you're welcome), but that first night together was so sweet. We were nervous and awkward, a little scared, but so excited. We'd honored one another and that in itself spoke volumes about our love. I was so glad we'd done the hard work of choosing purity—it made such a joyful difference in that wedding night! And while I had been totally focused on just that night for a long time (with unbelievable anticipation), the benefit of our decision lingers with us today. I love thinking about our wedding night. I *love* that we waited to go wild with each other. Holding off not only made a difference on that wedding night, it strengthened our marriage from that day forward. I didn't expect that, how living out purity would make a difference in other areas of our lives. But it not only benefited our individual spiritual journeys and our dating life, our marriage was blessed as a result of our choices.

Let's take a look at how that plays out for each one of us.

TRAINED FOR MARRIAGE

The temptation drove Joy nearly half crazy. She and her fiancé had made a commitment to purity and the closer they drew to the wedding day, the harder it was to keep their hands off of each other and their minds free of fantasizing. But they did it. They stuck their hands deep into their pockets, they hung out in public as often as possible, and they tried not to lose themselves in their good night kisses. It was nearly unbearable.

But they did it.

And not only did they make pure choices in their intimacy with each other, they guarded their conversation and the things they looked at, and did their very best to focus on their individual love relationships with their God.

"I knew that those choices would bless our marriage as far as intimacy and commitment," Joy said, "but I didn't realize that it was also training us for the years to come." Because Joy and Brett guarded their hearts and minds during their dating life, that purity muscle was strengthened for their marriage. Married for fifteen years now, they both say that it was the hard work they did in their dating relationship that equipped them for faithfulness and purity in marriage. "We were so dependent on God to help us fight temptation and make pure decisions," Brett said, "that our dependence translated right into our marriage relationship. Continued time with God gave us the strength to stand for each other, for faithfulness, and for pure devotion to one another—that was a benefit we never expected."

God is wise and good. He knew what he was doing when he called us to live out the pure identity he fought so hard to give us. You can always expect that obedience to him will be for your best—and will often bring about unexpected blessings.

TRUST IS BUILT

I had some trust issues before Brian and I married. I'd been betrayed in the past and I was scared that it would happen again. Like Brett and Joy, I knew that staying pure would bring a blessing to the physical connection in our marriage, but I never expected how it would help me work through areas damaged by broken trust. It began when Brian honored me throughout our dating—my trust and belief in him as a godly man grew.

After the wedding, a new dimension of that trust unfolded. Brian traveled for his work. Because he chose purity in our dating relationship, I knew I could trust him when he went on the road. What normally could have been a fearful thing for me—worry that someone would tempt him on the road—turned out to be just a small blip in my journey. I remember feeling the initial fear and then remembering, *Hey, he resisted his attraction for me and he was in love! Why would he give in to temptation with anyone else?*

Think of it. If you and your man make pure choices throughout your dating relationship, if you honor each other and guard your hearts, if you stay close to our God ... how much more will that build trust in marriage? If either one of you travels or if you end up in jobs with a lot of outside interaction, you will already know that your spouse is strong and secure regarding the area of purity—and as long as you both stay close to God and united to one another, no shadow of intimacy will ever be able to shake the real intimacy of your marriage relationship.

"Of course God tells us to live our lives pure, because his plan is for us to get married before we have children."
~Anna

ONE BODY, ONE PERSON

It is God's desire for each one of you that your first sexual experience be with your husband—and for your husband to experience his first touch of intimacy with you. He wants you to look deep into each other's eyes and feel the simmering passion. He delights in the thought of you delighting in each other. Sex is God's design and he meant for it to be an absolutely thrilling physical, emotional, and relational adventure for both husband and wife. To be one another's first is the most perfect outcome and God's original plan. I wish I could sit down with those of you who have the chance to see this happen in your life. I would sit with you over a warm cup of hot chocolate, look you in the eyes, and gently stress how fortunate you are. I would tell you what an amazing thing it is not to have to work though second chances ... that you are in the perfect position to know the complete blessing of moving into a marriage relationship without a single broken piece of unpure baggage to carry with you. While God restores and brings second chances, those of us with a broken history still carry memories and scars from previous sexual encounters. But not you. You have the chance to move forward without anything to work through ... What a treasure you have in your virginity! And what a gift you will be able to give the man of your dreams.

It makes me sad that I can't speak to this from a first-person perspective. I've spoken of the beauty of second chances, but I would like my friend, Louise, to share with you about what it meant for her to do this purity journey well.

What's the exciting part of a honeymoon, if it's not finally getting to be with the one you love?

Because my husband and I had saved ourselves for each other, we knew we had something special from the start. Oh my, we were both anxious and nervous our first time, but it was so exciting and special. Marriage was a whole new step, something totally different. If we had lived together or slept together before our wedding day, marriage would have been just more of the same.

It was a huge deal to know that neither one of us had been with anyone else. It was just us. I never had to wonder if he was comparing me to someone who was better or different. I didn't have anyone to compare him to either, so the pressure was off. It was as special as we made it because it was all about us.

My husband and I have been together thirty years and I have never had any reason to worry about anyone else—ever. Maybe it's because we were the first for each other and we trust each other completely. We know without a doubt that we will be together forever. That humbles me. Most people don't have that kind of trust. After all these years we both know that we still love each other and will always be there for each other. Even when things get rough, and they do, we know that we have each other and we will get through this life together. Our faith in Jesus and our decision to stay pure made a difference, and continues to make a difference in our marriage. It wasn't a decision that helped for a little while. It was a decision that has blessed us for years.

Choosing to live a pure life will benefit your marriage in so many ways. Whether it's saving yourself physically for marriage, guarding your eyes from broken images, or keeping close watch over your thoughts, each one of those decisions will ultimately bless your marriage relationship in ways beyond what you can imagine. Hold fast. Stand strong and pure. God has a best for you in this journey!

A SPECIAL NOTE

I want to take a minute to talk to those of you who may be skeptical about marriage. Maybe you came from a broken family, or you've seen enough ruined relationships that you've lost faith in all that marriage can be. If you're a child of divorce, it could be that you've determined never to marry, never to allow what happened to your parents to happen to you. I don't blame you.

There's no easy fix for what you feel. It's a tough thing to experience the pain of a broken family. It's hard to imagine that anything good can come out of marriage if all you've seen is broken promises and unhappy relationships. You are not wrong to feel that way. I imagine that's one of the reasons God says he hates divorce. Divorce harms not only the couple, but children and their future families ... and our God is brokenhearted over all that you've experienced.

But despite what you may hear or even see in your world, couples do make it—love can survive—and thrive. There are people who stand together for all their days, and are so grateful for each other. Listen to one child of divorce, Wendy, who has been blessed with a wonderful marriage:

As a child of divorce, I was afraid that it

just wasn't possible to stay married forever. I was afraid that I wouldn't be able to find someone who I could love, and who would love me back. I figured we'd get tired of each other or just stop loving each other after a certain number of years—nine, to be exact. I knew I'd need to date someone for at least nine years before I would know if I could stay with him, because my parents divorced after nine years.

Then I met John, and even in our dating relationship we put God first and focused on our relationship with him. As I kept my eyes on God, he confirmed that John was the one for me. And because of our individual love for God, our dating and our marriage relationship has been successful. We've been married now for twenty-five years. Oh girls, I can't tell you how excited I am that the cycle stopped with me! It is possible ...

Marriage is a wonderful thing, and because of God, the broken family of my childhood didn't become a broken family in my adulthood. The same can be true for you— the cycle of divorce can stop right here and now—in *your* life.

But the wisdom that comes from heaven is first of all pure; then peace-loving, considerate, submissive, full of mercy and good fruit.

James 3:17

Here's another story from a man married for nearly thirty years as he reflects on the beauty of marriage relationships:

One of the biggest lies our modern culture talks about is that newfound love is the best kind of love; that new discoveries are better than the old, familiar routines. [That] something fresh is better than something familiar. Everyone inevitably gets tired of the one they are with, right? So why commit to marriage? Why believe that marriage is even worth pursuing?

Well, the culture has it all wrong. The best kind of love is the love that works through the hardships of life together, sticks it out, and stays committed. And no matter your history, you can be one of those that sticks it out.

One of my favorite pictures of real love took place a number of years ago, when my dad was still alive. Mom and Dad were visiting for the holidays. My dad was extremely sick with the flu, and at one point he had a temp of 104.4. He was not speaking coherently and there were dirty tissues all over the bed. It was not a pretty picture. But I wish I could have captured the tender look of love in my mom's eyes when she wiped his brow and gave him his medication. She didn't see a sick man lying in a bed, she saw the love of her life, a love of fifty years, sick and in need of her care.

When my dad started to feel a little better, Mom brought him breakfast in bed. She gently woke him with a kiss and Dad, with sleepy eyes and a soft voice said, "I love seeing that face!"

I know that sounds like the kind of stuff you see only in movies. But I still tear up thinking about that scene.

That is what you get when you commit to lifelong love.

There is no shortcut for that.

Here's the truth: Even though you've known pain because of your parents or other broken relationships, that does not have to be your story. You can experience the real thing over the long haul—this is *your* life, and how it unfolds doesn't have to mirror any of the pain you've seen in your history.

One thing that will give you the added edge for a successful marriage is to make sure that you've dealt with your hurt from the divorce or broken relationships from your childhood. Don't be afraid to seek out help—books or Bible studies designed for children of divorce (*Unchained*, by Robyn Besemann, is one worth checking out). Resources are out there, and they can help you overcome your past so that it won't get in the way of the future our God has for you.

THE PURE MARRIAGE

The pure marriage can be your marriage. You can know the

total delight of loving God, trusting each other, and sharing life adventures together. Marriage isn't an easy ride, but going into it with pure choices will certainly give you the added strength to make it through the tough stuff. You'll have God's blessing, trust for one another, and a strengthened purity muscle to see you through temptation.

Fight through for pure choices. It's worth every cold shower and aching desire left unfulfilled to know the blessing of God-fulfilled desire just around the corner.

DISCUSSION/JOURNAL QUESTIONS

Can you see how choosing purity today will be a good thing for your marriage someday? Do future blessings strengthen you today? Why or why not?

If you could write a letter to your future husband about staying pure until you meet, what would you say? Let the words that you write encourage your own heart as well.

Do you believe that marriage is a good thing? What would be the benefits of becoming one with a man for the rest of your life? Write down every benefit you can think of.

If your heart has been broken by the loss of relationships around you, take a few moments to tell God about it and ask him to heal the hurt in your heart.

CHAPTER ELEVEN

KNOW YOUR STUFF

Answers to the questions you're asking

By this point, you've grappled with the reality of God's love and you've learned some of the benefits of purity and the consequences of impurity. You've tackled daily battles, what it looks like to date well, and how you can allow God to use technology as a positive force in your life. Finally, you looked at the beauty of a pure marriage, one of the sweetest benefits of choosing well. But there's more. As I was writing this book, I surveyed young women around the country, inviting girls to submit questions anonymously. Many of you took me up on it. I've tried to answer most of your questions throughout the book, but there were a few left unaddressed. So throughout this chapter I'll try to answer those questions, and also talk through how you can answer any question that might come up down the line—no matter the topic.

Where exactly does it say that we shouldn't have sex until we get married? I don't see that anywhere in Scripture.

The Bible doesn't have the words, "Don't have sex before

you're married" anywhere in its sixty-six books, but God addressed that topic from the very beginning in Genesis 2:24–25: First, a man leaves his father and mother, *then* he is united to his wife, and *then* they become one flesh.

The New Testament gets even further into the topic. In 1 Corinthians 7:8–9, the apostle Paul writes, "Now to the unmarried and the widows I say: It is good for them to stay unmarried, as I do. But if they cannot control themselves, they should marry, for it is better to marry than to burn with passion."

Paul talks of sex within marriage as if it is the only possible arena where passion can be explored. He doesn't say, "Hey, if you're single and burning with passion, go ahead and have sex." No, he makes it clear that passion unfolds in marriage, not outside of it.

The writer of Hebrews again talks about sex within the context of marriage: "Marriage should be honored by all, and the marriage bed kept pure, for God will judge the adulterer and all the sexually immoral" (13:4).

The writer says that God will judge the adulterer and all the sexually immoral. (In case you're wondering exactly what the verse is talking about, adultery is sex outside of marriage, and sexual immorality is—among other things— tied to sex before marriage.) This verse makes it very clear where sex takes place.

As a side note, you may feel uncomfortable with the words, "God will judge ..." That's okay. It's supposed to feel uncomfortable. It's like being a child living at home. If you blow off school or drink when you're under age or stay out past midnight, you'll hear about it. Why? Because your parents love you, set boundaries to protect you, and do all they can to make sure you live within those boundaries. Within those boundaries is where you're safest. God operates the same way. You harm yourself by having sex before marriage; you harm yourself and your spouse by having sex outside of marriage. God isn't going to turn aside from that. He'll look at it, judge it (call it sin), and confront our hearts. Why? Because he loves us and he knows what's best for us. Just like he will address the wrongs others commit against us, he will also address the wrongs we commit against our own bodies and against our relationship with him. That's what love does. It confronts broken things and helps us make things right.

Now keep in mind that you can ignore God's correction. You can feel him calling and then turn away and keep on doing what you're doing. You can also decide to bank on grace, and do what you want hoping to receive forgiveness later. If you do either of those things, God will never stop loving you, but he will let you walk away. He'll let you walk right into sin and keep on walking until you wonder how you ever got so far from his heart and so deep into the muck. But truly, why would you ever want to do that?

It's hard to believe that God wants us to remain virgins and then marry one person and live with them for the rest of our lives. If you look at the Old Testament, people got married to more than one person or slept around. What's up with that?

You're absolutely right! Scripture is full of people who made up their own rules. God made it very clear when he created the world that one man and one woman should marry. He talks of that man leaving his father and mother then uniting to his wife. He doesn't say "wives" or "wives and concubines." Unfortunately, as the years wore on, people created their own set of rules, even people who were followers of God. As a society, they determined it was okay to create a culture apart from God, so many people jumped on the bandwagon and decided to sleep with whomever they chose and take a few extra wives into their homes.

Did God stop loving them? No. But he let them walk away and he let them experience the consequences of their actions. When Abraham chose to sleep with his wife's handmaiden, God let him experience a domino effect of events that started a rebellious nation. When David chose to take a few extra brides to himself, he opened a door for a continuous battle with sexual brokenness. Even though David was a very godly man in other ways, he made a mess of things because of his temptations, and in time experienced consequences that included tremendous personal loss and heart-wrenching grief.

But these stories illustrate the beauty of the Bible. It's not a stuffy book that details the perfect lives of perfect people. It's the story of a world not much different from the way it is today. A world full of broken people and bad choices, but also a world filled with a passionate God who works out consequences for those he loves, one who constantly seeks the lost and loves with a fierce and passionate heart. Abraham still became the father of nations, and David still remained a man God called his own.

In Scripture you'll also find those who chose well and received pure blessing: Mary, the mother of Jesus; Daniel, who kept himself pure in every way and fought for his people. You'll also find those who made bad choices, dealt with the consequences, then moved forward into a life of pure devotion to their God and Savior: Peter, Paul, and David were men who followed that path. There were also those who went their own way completely, ignored God's corrections, and lost out: Cain, Esau, and Judas.

Read the Bible. Get to know the characters who look a whole lot like us. Get to know the God who remains the same, yesterday, today, and tomorrow, the one who holds you in his hand as firmly as he held the mother of Jesus. Don't let broken stories lead you to doubt; let those stories remind you how real the Bible is and how you, too, have a choice to either live pure (no matter your past) or to let past pain take you further away from God's gracious heart and the future he has for you. The choice is always yours.

I've heard girls say that they are "married" in the eyes of God so it's okay if they sleep with their boyfriends. How does that work?

It doesn't work. To be married in the eyes of God, you must be married in the eyes of the courts. You are not married until your marriage is official according to the authority of the land, and thus official according to the authority of God. If you hear someone say what they're doing is fine, remind them that God's eyes need to land on a marriage certificate before they will be "married in the eyes of God."

My best friend was a tomboy growing up and still thinks God made a mistake when he made her a girl. And then two of my friends say they're bisexual. They've told me that it's fine to experiment to figure out what they really want. All that stuff totally confuses me. What do you think?

I'm so grateful that I didn't grow up in today's world. I grew up with four older brothers and so I spent most of my early childhood wishing I were a boy. I was a full-fledged, no-doubt-about-it tomboy. I climbed trees, threw a football with a decent spiral, and lived a life about as adventurous as they come. In today's world, I might have been hauled into a psychiatrist's office. "Do you really feel like a boy?" "Yes," I would have said. "And I want to be one."

Well, after a flurry of tests and a close analysis of my torn-up jeans and propensity toward Matchbox cars, I may have been told that I actually was a boy trapped inside of a girl's body and therefore counseled to live as a boy from that point forward.

Now, I want to be careful here. I'm not discounting very real gender confusion. For me it was a stage I grew out of, but I know that for many young women this is a real struggle that has lasted into their teen years. If that's your story, I have nothing but deep compassion for you. I don't make light of your strong feelings, and I encourage you to seek godly counsel to help you navigate the questions and concerns you face every day. The most important truth you need to know is that God loves you and handcrafted you as a young woman. You are not a mistake. While societal pressures may pour into your life and encourage you to embrace a new identity, I encourage you to call out to the one who fashioned you. Hold on to the truth of his love and compassion. And talk to someone you trust who knows God's truth and loves you well. There's more to your story—don't let a broken society define what that looks like.

Here's the truth: it's a very normal thing to be a tomboy. If you've been one, or are one, it doesn't mean God made a mistake and you should have been born a boy. It's also a normal thing to find yourself, at some point in your life, attracted to someone of the same sex. Especially as women, we bond at the heart level. We get to know our best friends with fierce intimacy and deep devotion. Girls hold hands or lean against each other as they talk through the deep stuff of life. It's our nature to go to those places and to connect physically as we do … but it's so easy for a healthy friendship to turn into something it wasn't meant to be—simply because the idea was planted through mass media and cultural pressures. Because you've been inundated by your ability to choose, it can be easy to take a friendship into something more—even though that wasn't at all what God intended for you.

Don't get me wrong, the human body is beautiful. Both men and women are created with a unique brand of sexuality that can be very appealing and intriguing. I want you to know that an appreciation for feminine beauty does not mean that you are bisexual or homosexual. A phase where you find you have a crush on a girlfriend does not mean that you will forever be attracted to women. Our society is so quick to want to affirm sexual choices that it can twist untrustworthy feelings into forever lifestyles, robbing young women of what God longs to do in their future. Be very cautious in listening to the lying voices of a broken world.

If this has been an area of struggle for you, if any of these things touched a cord in your heart, I want to encourage you again to call out to our God and talk with someone you trust. There's so much more to the issues than I can cover in these pages, so please go to someone you consider safe, godly, and authentic. This is not something you should walk through alone, and please remember, there is no shame in the battles you are waging—our God is more than able to work through it all as you seek his counsel.

What about masturbation? Is that a good alternative to having sex?

It seems like the ideal solution, right? You're not hurting anyone else. You are releasing all that pent-up sexual tension and you are free to interact with your boyfriend without going crazy with longing.

The problem is, nothing could be further from the truth. Let's dissect that statement one lie at a time:

I'M NOT HURTING ANYONE ELSE.

Oh, but you are … in a few different ways. First, you hurt your future husband. If you masturbate, you become the expert in pleasing yourself. You know where and how to touch yourself to bring the most pleasure. Your man will never be able to compete. You'll find that you won't enjoy the intimacy of your married life nearly as much because you'll be accustomed to sexual release in one certain way. You also harm others by using them to stimulate your mind. Very rarely can you pleasure yourself without picturing another person. That means you're using someone for purely selfish purposes. God calls us to love and honor one another, and not to lust after each other. Masturbation is a direct expression of that lust—which hurts you and hurts God's heart as a result.

BUT IT'S A RELEASE OF SEXUAL TENSION.

Ummm, no. Masturbation actually increases sexual tension. If you've spent an evening fantasizing and pleasing yourself, the next day your sexual antenna will be up. You'll notice people's bodies more. The images that occupied your mind the night before will spill into your day. You'll find yourself all the more consumed with thoughts and images as you go about your daily life. It can easily grow into an addictive behavior that never satisfies.

IT WILL HELP MY BOYFRIEND AND ME STAY PURE—IT WILL TAKE CARE OF THE LONGING.

Again, not true. If you visualized you and your boyfriend having sex, that image will be in your brain the next time you spend time together. You'll be much more primed to see if the fantasy matches up to the real-life experience. Think about it, ladies. If you've already gone there in your brain, it will make it that much easier to cross the line in person.

Our culture is selling you a false bill of goods. They will tell you that you have to have some kind of "release" every so often to stay healthy and sane. People who don't have sex or don't engage in any kind of sexual behavior are pictured as uptight, cranky, and moody.

The exact opposite is true. Masturbation never satisfies. What might begin as a once-in-a-while experience can quickly turn into an addiction that needs to be fed greater and greater doses of broken lust. In other words, as the images that first stimulated you (sex with your boyfriend) fail to satisfy, the images you seek out become more and more broken and deviant. Pretty soon you'll find yourself reading stories or going online to stir up the same level of sexual arousal. Talk about uptight, cranky, and moody—those are exactly the emotions that will come as you seek to fill yourself with something so empty that it will never satisfy.

Do you remember how we looked at purity as freedom in the first chapter? Purity *is* freedom. Freedom from shame. Freedom from addiction. Freedom from pursuits that only add shame and heartache to your pure lives.

Don't listen to those who tell you masturbation is a healthy alternative to sex. Don't let the shame of this particular addiction wrap its tentacles around you. If you haven't gone there, stay away from it. If you have gone there and you're feeling regret, go to our God and ask for his help in dealing with the temptation. Remind yourself of the truths we just talked about, and if you need to, invite some accountability into your life. Finally, if this is part of your life and you are feeling resistance to my words, thinking, *She doesn't know what she's talking about. It's not that big of a deal*, just ask God to show you the harmful effects. Ask him to give you eyes to see how this choice is harming you or how it's harmed others. Don't just take my word for it.

My friend and I have committed to living a pure life. Now she is dating and I have a feeling she and her boyfriend have crossed some major lines. Is there anything I can do? I feel like she's making big mistakes, but I don't know how I can help her.

It's so hard to see someone you love making a decision that will hurt them. The good thing is, you can help your friend in some important ways. Since you've made a commitment to standing together in purity, it's important that you talk with her. Come alongside her in love and let her know that you have nothing but her best at heart. Be careful that you don't condemn her, but gently remind her of the promise she made and the reason she made the promise in the first place. Take her back to the truth of God's love and his desire for her best. If she seems open to your words, dive in deeper and talk about the risks she is taking and encourage her to go to God with the choices she's made. Offer to go with her in prayer. If she's willing, walk through the process of returning to God's heart and offer to help keep her accountable in her relationship. That would be the ideal scenario—where she admits to poor choices and chooses to make it right and stay accountable.

Unfortunately, it doesn't often happen that way. You can come alongside her and talk with her, but if she refuses to listen or seems unwilling to hear your heart, the only choice you have is to pray. Go to our God and bring her choices to him. Bring her to his feet and ask God to intervene. As you pray, keep an eye out for the opportunity to again speak truth in love. Fight for her on your knees and whenever you have the chance, fight for her in person.

The pure life can be hard, and so you definitely need your friends in these battles. You need each other to help see truth, to pray, and to go to bat when you feel weak. If you have a friend who is making poor choices, do what you can to speak truth, and if she doesn't receive it, take her to our God and be prepared to love her when she faces the harsh consequences of her decisions.

THE BEST ANSWER TO EVERY QUESTION

I know I've only scraped the surface of the real-life sexual issues you face every day. Other things will come into your world as the days unfold—or they may have already. You'll have questions and thoughts and worries about any number of different things. Because of that, I want to not only answer some of your questions, but point you to a method of answering them yourself. There's a sure-fire method to finding out God's truth in the midst of this culture. If you are confused, or you have additional questions, try these things to find the answer:

ASK

First, ask God. Talk to him. Sure, it's good to ask people and read books to figure out what God might possibly think or want from us, but we also have to remember that our God is a good God, a loving Father who promises to be found as we seek him. So call out to him and share your confusion, question, or concern. Ask him to reveal truth to you in a way that you will be able to see and understand.

GO TO THE BIBLE

So first you ask, then you go to God's love letter to you. It talks of this grand, romantic journey God took to bring people to his heart. Every chapter is another picture of his truth, grace, and power. Go there. If it feels intimidating, talk to someone who has been studying the Bible for a long time, who is passionate about it and excited to share that passion. My friend Jennifer is crazy about the Bible. When I used to feel overwhelmed by all the stories or when I had a hard time connecting the dots, Jennifer showed me how God worked, how his love wove through the Old Testament and into the New. I needed to learn from someone who knew more than me so that I could begin to figure it out on my own—Jennifer provided that teaching. You can do the same thing. Go to someone who is knowledgeable and passionate about the Bible. Ask them to show you more about God and his love through its pages. Then, when you have a question, it will be easier to go to the Bible and find the answer. As you read, look at his heart and his character, see the way he worked in the lives of his people, and go from there. For example, it might not say in Scripture, "Do not masturbate," but it does say not to lust, to honor others, and to guard your heart. It also talks of God's love and his desire for you to have a pure heart so that you can see God and enjoy that love relationship on a daily basis. Because of that, you can draw the conclusion that God wants you to avoid masturbating.

Also, knowing God's truth will be your strength when someone comes at you with a Bible verse that seems out of line. Some people will take a verse and twist it so that it looks nothing like real truth. As you know more about the Bible, you'll be better able to figure things out based on what you've learned, and you'll be able to toss aside anything that doesn't match what you know of God. If you don't dive into the Bible, it will be easy to get a mixed-up image of who God really is and what he wants for your life. Go to his love letter. He wants to speak to you through the Bible.

TALK TO GODLY PEOPLE

After you ask God to show you the truth and go to the Bible to find out what he's saying, then talk with someone who knows her stuff. A godly person is one who loves God, holds fast to the Bible, and lives his or her faith. Hopefully, you'll find some of those people in your church, in your youth group, or in your school. Wherever you find them, take time to connect with them and build those relationships. It will be those people who will remind you of why you're fighting the temptations, of who God is and how much he loves you, and they'll be the ones to pray for you when you're feeling overwhelmed. That's why it's so important to be plugged into a group of people who are hungry after God's heart; when you have questions, you can go to the Bible and then go to people you trust and ask them. Finally, if there is any way that we can help, we'd love to do that. Visit *www.purelovepurelife.com* and you'll find a section called "Ask Away." If we don't know the answer to your question, we'll do our best to figure it out. Remember, we're all in this together—for the long haul.

God loves deep thinkers and question-askers. He wants you to have a faith that is real and vibrant and based in truth. Don't be afraid to give everything you have to find out who he is and what he thinks.

DISCUSSION/JOURNAL QUESTIONS

As you read through this chapter, is there a particular question that stuck out as one you've asked? Which one? Do you feel like your question was answered? Why or why not?

Do you have a friend that is struggling in the area of purity right now? Have you talked with her? What is one step you can take to remind her of God's desire for purity?

Do you feel like you know a lot about God's character through the Bible? Is there a way get to know God better? What is one step you can take to make that a reality going forward?

CHAPTER TWELVE

SAYING YES

Amazing passions to pursue

Mariah couldn't remember the last time she felt this good. She felt like she was really starting to get it. But, oh, what a ride it had been—she'd been boy crazy for so long, she didn't think she'd ever move past it. Ever since she met Paul in the third grade and he chased her around the playground for that kiss, she'd been smitten. Of course after Paul there was Austin, Luke, Curran, and Andrew ... and that was just in the fourth grade! And so it went. Mariah spent the next ten years completely consumed with the next guy in her life.

Things were different now, and Mariah had never felt so free. It's not that she didn't think about guys, it's just they didn't consume her every thought. She didn't fight the daily temptation to connect to someone, *anyone*, and she felt absolutely no desire to make the compromises she used to make on a regular basis.

The pure teen. Confident, secure, settled in her love for Jesus. Imagine a life so consumed with good and so full of love that desperation and desire lose their grip on your choices.

No matter your history, this can be your future. As you

walk with God, get to know him, and experience his love, pure living can be your reality. And while there are many things we've talked about regarding how to guard your heart, mind, and body, purity is also about the stuff you can do, the good things you can enjoy.

So let's take a look at some of the things you can say yes to in order to embrace this radical, pure, and powerful life that lies ahead:

It takes one passion to conquer another.

SAYING YES TO GOOD RELATIONSHIPS

It was late and full-blown goofiness had set in. Samantha had just finished putting fifteen different braids in Rebecca's hair. "I look like I've sprouted roots," Rebecca said with a laugh.

"You should leave them in all night and see what your hair looks like in the morning."

"Knowing my luck, I'll never be able to get them out!"

"Perfect!"

Rebecca smiled with a glint in her eye, "Your turn now." Samantha had hair down to her bottom. "We should only need about sixty hair ties to finish it off …"

Hair ties. Ice cream. Movies and a few air mattresses. It was a perfect night of simply hanging out, and Rebecca's heart was full. She loved Samantha and her friend's wacky sense of humor. She loved staying up all night and talking about nothing of any great importance. She loved not thinking about school, parents, guys, or anything else for that matter. This was girl time, and it was just what the doctor ordered.

Pure living is all about enjoying pure relationship. It's connecting to people who share your values and enjoy having a blast together. Sure, there's a time and a place for deep spiritual discussions, but living a pure life with people you love is not defined by how serious you are together. Embracing pure loving and pure living is all about the fun you can have with friends and family. God created this world as a playground, and gave us the best toys and pleasures to enjoy. If you live near the water, you can go splash in the waves with your friends. If you live in the mountains, you can climb on the rocks and explore the caverns with family. No matter where you live, you can spend your time enjoying pure pursuits with people you love—developing authentic relationships that will last a lifetime.

FUN GIRLFRIENDS

Build face-to-face relationships with other teens. If you have a few good girlfriends who share your love for Jesus, be intentional in taking time with them. If you don't have those kinds of friendships in your life, you can take steps to build them. Show up at youth group or at a high school or college fellowship. Sit next to someone who has a contagious smile and introduce yourself. It starts there, and it grows as you commit to those group environments. Building friendships isn't as hard as you might think.

Once you make those connections, take time to have fun. Watch movies together, go for hikes, get outside, or just sit and visit. So often our poor choices come out of loneliness and isolation, so build relationships with people you enjoy.

Laugh, cry, play. God created us to be in real relationship. Enjoy your friends and watch how God loves you through one another's hearts.

GOOD FAMILY TIME

Family? It's true. As you get older, your family—from brothers and sisters to parents, aunts, uncles, and grandparents—will become more and more important to you. Take time with them now. Show an interest in their worlds. Have you ever asked your grandmother what she wanted to be when she grew up? About her first crush or what it was like to live with her parents? Have you ever asked your dad about what kind of superhero he admired, or why he chose the career he did? What about your brothers and sisters? I know they may drive you crazy today, but they are some of the few people who will know you from birth through death. They are the only ones who saw you run around in your diapers and will likely visit you in a nursing home. It's easy to take those relationships for granted but what if you took some time building them instead? Take a few minutes to find out who your brother has a crush on (as a way to connect instead of to tease him) or what your sister dreams of becoming. Take your cousin out for coffee or show up at her basketball game. You have a unique opportunity to invest in relationships that will forever be a part of your world, no matter what. You will never regret time you've given to family.

GREAT DATING RELATIONSHIPS

I just want to stress again that living out this pure life doesn't mean you run from dating or lock yourself up in some sort of convent. The beauty of living the pure life is that you can have a blast in a healthy dating relationship without worrying about all the junk that can come with pushing the boundaries on purity. Remember, God loves a good romance, he knows how good it feels for us to enjoy flowers, dinners, dates, good-night kisses. He's the one that wired us so we would enjoy all of that!

So don't be afraid to enjoy meeting guys, talking to them on the phone, letting a relationship build through friendship, conversation, banter, and play. Enjoy the process—the anticipation that builds when you're going to see him, getting ready and feeling the butterflies, hearing the doorbell ring and knowing it's him... enjoy every heart-pounding moment of a fun romantic relationship.

That's the beauty of purity—it actually enhances an already good thing. It makes dating even better, more exciting, more mysterious and alluring. God knew what he was doing when he called us to purity, he knew what we needed, but also what we'd love.

Don't be afraid to enjoy a good dating relationship. God's in the middle of that pleasure too.

SAYING YES TO FUN PHYSICAL ACTIVITIES

Mary loved the way she felt after basketball practice. She hated having to do planks, but she loved the sprints, shooting, and the way her body felt after a hard workout. She especially loved her team: Jan with her crooked smile and spiked hair; Anna and her awkward three pointers where it never looked like the ball was actually going to go in, and then *swoosh*. Every time.

Mary loved cheering on her friends and loved being

cheered on. It felt good to be part of something bigger than herself.

GET PHYSICAL

Sports, dance, working out: they are all healthy outlets to release energy and build pure community. In fact, not too long ago, I took my own advice and tried Zumba. The women in the class had a ton of rhythm and looked so beautiful, and I wanted to be like them. Unfortunately, I don't seem to have the gift of Zumba coursing through my veins—my hiney wiggles to its own beat.

It wasn't pretty—but I still had a blast and my body was exhausted afterward.

Exercising for a purer life may sound strange, but trust me it takes more than a cold shower to deal with the physical longings that can sometimes sweep in. Most of you know that if you focus on *not* feeling the longing, you'll just feel the longing even more. So rather than focus on not wanting to touch your boyfriend, or not feeling a physical desire, it's definitely a better route to replace that longing with a positive outlet. Get outside. Go running. Join a fitness class. Join a pick-up basketball team. You don't have to be great at sports to find fun physical activities. Try dancing (not where you're pressed up against a guy, by the way), and get some of that physical energy redirected.

It would be a big fat lie to say that once you've embraced pure living you won't ever feel a physical longing again. Those moments will come, but God is so good and so faithful. He says that there will be temptation, but he promises to give you a way out (1 Corinthians 10:13). Exercise is one of those ways.

Take a few minutes right now and think about what kind of physical activities you like. Hiking? Skiing? Running? Dancing? How can you work it into your schedule? Figure it out and make it happen. You'll be surprised how much it will help keep your mind focused on good things and relieve you of the physical longings and temptations.

SAYING YES TO TOUCH

Everybody needs touch. This reality is proven in orphanages around the world: Babies who are held and cuddled gain weight, eat well, and smile more. Babies who aren't held tend to struggle in their physical development and overall health.

So please know the truth. Your need for touch is a very real need, and understanding that reality means you can be smart in meeting that need in healthy ways.

Here's how it works: hug your friends, wrap your arms around your mom. You could even get a puppy or a cat, guinea pig or ferret. Not a goldfish though—not nearly cuddly enough. In my youth group years, we were big on back rubs. Everybody would get in a circle and rub each other's shoulders. I was always the first one to jump on that bandwagon and the last one to want to leave. I loved it.

We all need good, healthy touch, to connect with another living being who thinks we're wonderful. So be intentional in finding healthy people who are safe, or get a puppy or kitten of your own that will snuggle up beneath your chin.

It's better to be intentional and seek out healthy touch than not to recognize the need and end up going after touch that will leave you facing painful consequences.

SAYING YES TO FEELINGS

I should always have a box of tissues with me when I go into a movie theater. Especially when I know the storyline is going to tug at my heart. Even the animated movies where the dog fights off the mountain lion to save his little master or the alien gets all attached to his human friends but then has to head back to his alien hometown … I love that stuff. To get lost in a good story is one of my favorite things. And even though I pretend not to cry and fiercely wipe away any evidence before the lights come up, the reality is that I'm a sucker for a great story.

Good movies, great books, inspiring shows: these are healthy and pure outlets to express God-given emotions. It's completely human to enjoy getting lost in feelings that stir your soul. Even a great love song or romantic comedy can be a wonderful thing—but instead of letting those things build your yearning for a guy, let them remind you of God's love. When you hear a love song, let it remind you of your God's heart. Now before you dismiss this advice, hear me out. I can remember my big brother listening to a love song that I'd attached to a guy in my life. "I love that song," he said. "Anytime I hear it, I sing it to God." I thought he was weird when he first told me that, but every time I heard the song after that, I would belt it out … and think of God.

So yes, we've talked about the reality that there is a lot of trash out there to avoid, but it doesn't mean you should never read a book, watch a movie, or listen to music. God is creative. He is the author of the arts. He uses beauty, music, and adventure to stir the hearts of his people. (Want proof? Just read the Scriptures and you'll find all kinds of stories of heroes and villains and true love.) So rather than allowing your emotions to get lost in a relationship or stirred toward physical passion, use healthy avenues to feel and express those same emotions in ways that will keep you safe.

Dear friends, now we are children of God, and what we will be has not yet been made known. But we know that when Christ appears, we shall be like him, for we shall see him as he is. All who have this hope in him purify themselves, just as he is pure.

1 John 3:2–3

SAYING YES TO GOD

Mallory put on her headphones, threw on a light jacket, and headed for the door. She loved running in the early evening so she could catch the splash of colors as the sun settled over the Missouri countryside. She turned on some of her favorite worship music, turned it up loud, and let her feet fall into a steady rhythm. She loved being out here, just her and God and the music—it was her favorite part of the day.

WILD WORSHIP

Worship doesn't have to look a certain way. You are wired with a unique and beautiful voice, and God wants to hear from you. A few songs on Sunday morning may not be your thing. Maybe you're an artist or a writer or a photographer. Maybe you love the outdoors and you feel closest to God when you're hiking a trail. While it's important for you to be plugged into a church of good and kind believers, you can worship God in lots of different ways. If you're a writer, you can take some time and write to him what you love. If you paint or draw, you can turn on some music and draw your heart for God, painting colors and beauty onto the page. If you're a singer, sing. If you're a dancer, dance. You are beautiful in God's sight and he wants to hear your unique voice calling out to him. Whatever it looks like. The beautiful thing about worship is that it connects you to God's heart. You think you're praising him but you walk away feeling like he has just poured out love all over you. Things change in worship. *You* change in worship.

Love your God and let him love you.

Those who live according to the flesh have their minds set on what the flesh desires; but those who live in accordance with the Spirit have their minds set on what the Spirit desires. The mind governed by the flesh is death, but the mind governed by the Spirit is life and peace.

Romans 8:5–6

REAL RELATIONSHIP

Yes, it's great to go to the Bible to find answers to your questions, but it's just as wonderful to go there to find out more about the one you love. It's like reading a biography of a loved one, finding out what he likes and thinks about, discovering his interests and passions. Take time every day to read a little bit about the one who loves you most. Ask yourself what the verses say about your God and what that means for your life. Let those verses become a part of you.

LOOK OUT FOR OTHERS

As you read about God and find out about the things that matter to him, you discover there's one really big thing on his mind: people. Hurting people. And you—no matter your story, no matter your past, no matter where you are today— have a role to play in reaching out to those hurting people. God wants you to be part of their story. Sure, he could do it without you. He could plant a little burning bush outside of everyone's front door and extend a very personal invitation to each life. He could show up as an angel to each and every person and make himself known. Instead, he lets us be a part of one another's stories. We get to show another person Jesus, and then we get to experience the joy in knowing that somehow, someway, we just did something for good in this world. There is no better feeling! So try reaching out to someone in your circle today—it could be someone who is financially poor or spiritually poor. You could give them a piece of yourself. Find your place in their story and then live it out. You'll be amazed at how much you are blessed in return, how much dimple-cratering joy you'll feel.

Jesus said it this way: "My food is to do the will of him who sent me ..." (John 4:34). Nothing made Jesus happier than filling the role God had given to him. You will experience the same. As you find out the things you are good at— whether you're a great listener, an encourager, a teacher, or a behind-the-scenes servant—use those gifts and watch what God does in your heart as a result.

DREAM BIG

Life is big, there's so much ahead for you. Yes, it's easy to pour all your time and energy into the next crush, into online relationships, into feeding physical desire, but think of what could happen if you poured that same energy into dreaming about what you want to do with your life? You can take steps to fulfill those dreams now, instead of waiting until you're older.

Dream big. If you could do anything in the world, what would you do? What stirs your joy? What drives you crazy? What steps can you take to make the world a better place today? You are beautiful, God loves you so much, and there's something you bring to this planet that no one else brings; your experiences, heart, talent, emotion—the world is better with you in it. What fun to figure out your role in the big story God is writing with all of us!

Don't let anyone look down on you because you are young, but set an example for the believers in speech, in conduct, in love, in faith and in purity.

1 Timothy 4:12

God has grand adventures for you, a hope and a future … If you are a willing heart (and he searches for willing hearts), he can do mighty things through you. And there is no better feeling than knowing the God of the universe just put you into his story as one of his most cherished characters.

Dream big. Love big. Live pure.

For other big ideas, check out *www.purelovepurelife. com*: Click on "Saying yes …", where you'll find a whole bunch of options of things you can say *yes* to, including being part of ministries that were either started by teens or started in honor of teens who are in heaven now. Early on in the book I told you about my nephew Caleb and how he was in a car accident—my brother and his wife started the Caleb Foundation, which reaches out to orphans around the world. Other ministries deal with abolishing human slavery or providing clean water or helping young girls rescued from the sex trade—check it out and join in. And if you start your own ministry, let us know. This is about helping each other pour passion into healthy outlets and dream big dreams. Let's do this together!

SAYING YES TO LOVE

When I was dating Brian, I worked in an office environment. It was a quiet place, full of cubicles and editor-type people. I'd come back from lunch with Brian and drive everyone around me nuts. I'd whistle, laugh out loud for no real reason, turn on my iTunes and tap my feet to an annoying love song. Wow, did they get sick of me.

But I was in love! Crazy about my man and not afraid to let everyone know.

And that was a human guy—a great human guy, but still human.

When I was younger, I would talk about a guy like he was absolutely the best thing ever. I'd go to my mom or my best friend and fill her in on all his amazing traits. "He's got a great smile, amazing eyes, he's funny ..." I'd talk about his potential. "He'll probably end up saving all the children in Africa one day," I'd say. Or, "I'm pretty sure he's going to be the one to bring world peace."

But listen to this guy:

> He is the Maker of heaven and earth,
> the sea, and everything in them—

> he remains faithful forever.
> He upholds the cause of the oppressed
> and gives food to the hungry.
> The Lord sets prisoners free,
> the Lord gives sight to the blind,
> the Lord lifts up those who are bowed down,
> the Lord loves the righteous.
> The Lord watches over the foreigner
> and sustains the fatherless and the widow.
>
> Psalm 146:6–9

Okay, so I would go crazy over a nice smile—meanwhile, God is faithful forever, watches out for people, feeds the hungry, sets prisoners free, gives sight to the blind, watches over the fatherless. And guess what? He actually *is* the one who will bring world peace!

Now that's a God worth falling in love with, a God worth serving with all our hearts, a God worth fighting for ... and when we feel loved by a God like that, we'll do more than play love songs in a cubicle world. We'll do more than drive people nuts with our in-love grin and random laughter. We'll be contagious, vibrant, goofy in all the best ways and full of life. We'll be drop-dead gorgeous whether we have a bit of makeup on or not. That's what love does; that's what pure love does in a heart willing to receive it.

Some people say that you need to live a pure life to know pure love. It's actually the other way around. When you know pure love, when you know the deep, amazing love of a God who is real and amazing in every way, the pure life will come.

You're doing it, girl. You're letting God love you and loving him back, loving others and running from sexual temptation, you're fighting the good fight of purity—and in the process, you're becoming more and more beautiful, more and more contagious, pure, bold, and adventurous. I'm proud of you. Don't give up, don't give in.

What a ride this will be!

DISCUSSION/JOURNAL QUESTIONS

Do you feel like you have good relationships with family and friends? What is one thing you can do to either build those relationships or continue to build them? Be specific.

As you think about healthy physical outlets, what appeals to you? Do you enjoy hiking? Biking? Walking? Dancing? How can you incorporate that into your life in the coming weeks?

Just for fun, what is the best movie you've seen recently? Can you see how love stories and adventure movies can draw you to God's heart? Why or why not?

What is one step you can take to build your love relationship with God? Spend time in wild worship? Get to know him through the Bible? Think of one step you can take and how you can follow through in the coming week.

DO YOU KNOW JESUS?

Jesus. Maybe you've heard about him, but you don't really know him. Maybe you've even grown up in the church, but you haven't made your relationship personal. This is your chance. See, this is how it all came to pass: God is perfect. Totally perfect. He is as pure and clean as the driven snow. He can't be around sin. It's not that he doesn't want to be around it, he literally can't. It's like oil and water—God and sin just don't mix. So before God could interact with people, the sin had to be wiped away. The only way the sin could be taken care of was by a sacrifice. In the Old Testament, an animal could pay the price ... but people kept right on sinning—which meant another sacrifice, and another and another. It was an endless cycle that kept God from really interacting and relating with the people he loved so much.

So God came up with a plan. Jesus. His perfect Son, his boy, flesh of his flesh, would go down to earth. Jesus would live a perfect life and give that life up as the perfect sacrifice, the once-and-for-all price paid for sin. Not just your sin, but your great-grandfather's sin and the sin of your great grandbaby. One sacrifice, once and for all. And then to make it even easier, all we have to do is admit that we don't have it together, that we've sinned (easy enough for most of us to admit), and then choose to believe that Jesus was God's Son and that he paid the price for us. It's that simple and that huge, all at the same time. Think of what God could have done: He could have made us follow a zillion rules, he could have had us write our choices a thousand times on a heavenly chalkboard, or had us climb the highest mountain on our knees to prove how sorry we were. But instead he simply tells us to admit that we don't have it together, believe that Jesus paved the way, and then do our part to build our love relationship with our God. Once we take that step, Jesus comes into our life, and when God looks at us he now sees the perfect heart and life of his Son. He can relate to us and spend time with us because the sin of our past, present, and future is covered up by Jesus's sacrifice. It's an amazing exchange—Jesus's perfection for our brokenness. Mind-boggling and beautiful …

If you don't know Jesus, it's easy to take the first step. Tell him that you don't have it together, make a choice to believe in all that he did for you, and let him know you can't wait to get to know him, to experience his love and to live in relationship with him. This is an opportunity to build a relationship with the living God who is totally and completely crazy about you. Go for it. Really. Say your first prayer right here and now, and ask God to come into your life. He'll do it … and as you get to know him, love him, and live for him, it will change everything.